POETOPIA

AROUND THE WORLD

Edited by Jenni Bannister

First published in Great Britain in 2015 by:

Remus House
Coltsfoot Drive
Peterborough
PE2 9BF
Telephone: 01733 890066
Website: www.youngwriters.co.uk

Book Design by **ASHLEY JANSON**

SB ISBN 978-1-78443-586-8

Printed and bound in the UK by BookPrintingUK
Website: www.bookprintinguk.com

FOREWORD

Welcome, Reader!

For Young Writers' latest competition, Poetopia, we gave secondary school pupils nationwide the challenge of writing a poem based on the rules of one of 5 factions: Castitas for reflective, honest poetry; Temperantia for angry, assertive poetry; Humilitas for positive, uplifting poetry; Benevolentia for emotional poetry; and Industria for diligent, structured poetry. Poets who wrote a poem outside of these parameters were assigned to Dissimĭlis.

We chose poems for publication based on style, expression, imagination and technical skill. The result is this entertaining collection full of diverse and imaginative poetry, which is also a delightful keepsake to look back on in years to come.

Here at Young Writers our aim is to encourage creativity in the next generation and to inspire a love of the written word, so it's great to get such an amazing response, with some absolutely fantastic poems. Once all the books in the series are published we will pick the best poem from each faction to win a prize.

I'd like to congratulate all the young poets in **Poetopia - Around the World** - I hope this inspires them to continue with their creative writing. And who knows, maybe we'll be seeing their names on the best seller lists in the future...

Jenni Bannister

Jenni Bannister
Editorial Manager

THE FACTIONS

CASTITAS (Kas-ti-tas)

- Write a soul-baring, honest poem
- Tell us what it is like to be you
- Channel your confusion and emotions at being a teenager into verse

TEMPERANTIA (Temper-ran-tee-ah)

- Stand up for someone or something
- Vent your anger through poetry
- Express your frustration about a situation that's out of your control

HUMILITAS (Hu-mil-lih-tahs)

- Write a positive, uplifting poem
- Write an ode to celebrate someone or something that you appreciate
- Write a spiritual poem

BENEVOLENTIA (Ben-e-vol-en-tee-ah)

- Write a love / emotional poem
- Empathise with another's situation or predicament
- Write a praise poem
- Write a poem about your best friend / your friendship

INDUSTRIA (In-dust-ree-ah)

- Write a poem about current affairs
- Use a strict poetic form, such as a sonnet or kyrielle
- Research a poet of your choice and write in a similar style

DISSIMĬLIS (Diss-i-mĭl-is)

- If pupils write a poem that falls outside of the factions' rules, they become Dissimĭlis
- Poems can be on any theme or style

CONTENTS

THE POEMS

Tears For No One

We cry in secret, from whom do we hide?
Why are we ashamed?
Is it because we fear that our emotions will be exploited
Or that we show emotion at all?
Perhaps we should yell until our throats are red and raw instead,
And our voices disintegrated.

We should claw at our flesh,
As if unleashing an unholy beat.
God should not tear the sky apart as if he knows,
But should make it dark and cloudy out of respect.
Every man, woman and child,
Every angel should stop and cry those glistening tears.

They should scream and claw,
Run and beg and pray.
Anything to alter the thought of what may happen.
What is happening
And what has already happened?
Because I did.

Nevertheless . . .
Cars drive and crash and burn.
People rush defiant and uncaring in the street.
The sun continues to shine unfeeling, steely light.
And I silently sob in my own dark corner,
A perfect stranger and a secret to the world outside.

Though even I will forget,
For all things must come to an end, good and bad.
Stubbornly, I do not want to neglect the pain or the numbness.
The varied emotion that fed my bitterness.

How am I to be blamed for the corruption of my face?
Is it not in divinity's name we disgrace?
More for *his* chosen ones,
The ones that accept his true love.
The drink of angels,
They shed human tear.

Shakira Chowdhury (14)

High Ambitions

I reach for the sky
But sometimes wonder why
Do I want attention?
Hoping my name will be mentioned?
My heart begins to race
You can see the worried look on my face
Will I pull this off
Or will all my hard work be lost?
As I step forward with a smile to present
I hide the fear, this isn't my best event
I fly, I jump, I spin, I leap
I know this is the best feeling I could reap
Regardless of my place, I finish with a smile
As I know it was all worthwhile
The blood, the sweat, the pain, the tears
The dedication, the sacrifice all the years
It all leads up to days like today
When after the word 'gold', my name they say.

Beth Lauren Berry (13)

Revelations Of A Bookworm

Books are strange.
They're like portals to other worlds.
You just need to read a page
And suddenly you're drowning in words.

They can have hidden message with lessons
Or be made simply to entertain.
Down you go on the waterfall of letters,
No two stories are quite the same.

They broaden your mind
And make you laugh or cry.
Authors become gods of their own creations,
Making characters striking, bold or shy.

Jessica Fraser (13)

Thoughts

Negative thoughts are surrounding me.
They're like thick clouds that hide my ability to see
All the beauty and happiness there is in a day,
I wish I could just blow them away.

The thought of inevitable death dawns on me.
I mean, there's still so much for me to see,
What if I don't fulfil my life purpose
Or I don't have one and I'm just worthless?

Not being good enough is something I constantly worry about.
Being smart and pretty enough is something I doubt.
Every time I walk about the street,
I compare myself to other girls that I'll never meet.

These thoughts are never pretty,
Maybe I'm just in a vortex of self-pity,
'Help, help,' I scream and shout
As I try to find a way to get out.

Zoe Lee (13)

I Love You The Most

Every day, the first thing I want to see is your eyes,
Without you I'm nothing.
Whenever you're here my heart flies,
You are life, my peace and you alone are my love.
You mean the world to me,

You're the best thing that happened to me.
You make me feel so special,
You always had been there for me.
You're the one I love
And no matter what, I will forever keep loving you.

Mohammed Chowdhury

Rays Of Light

Over the hill the sun peeks out,
Warm and gleaming,
Darkness without,

Its rays spill over the countryside,
Over the beaches,
Over the tide,

The warmth and brightness of the sun,
Brings day to some animals,
Night for some,

The sun can be looked at in many ways,
But don't let it blind you,
By its rays,

When darkness falls, the sun is out of sight,
As the stars light up,
To bid a goodnight.

Charlotte Victoria Burkert

Winter's Night

Darkness arrives and so does the cold
Inside the house the heating goes on
Sheets are pulled over people
Soft fluffy blankets as well
In the house there is no sound
Mice squeak all through the night
In the middle of the night some people wake
Lights outside flicker on and off
In the house alarms go off
Sun comes up and people wake.

Zoe Williamson (13)

My Best Friend

True friends are hard to find,
But there you are you came into my life.
You came to me in a perfect time,
I'm so happy you're a friend of mine.

We'll always be friends,
We'll be buddies till the end,
We've got each other's back
And we'll stay on the right track.

We love this song,
Because we always sing along.
We always do a pose,
This is how it goes . . .

F is for friends, who do stuff together,
U is for 'u' and me,
N is for no, nowhere to go, down in the deep blue sea!

Rayyan Chowdhury (9)

Me

My thoughts are a roller coaster at its climax
My feelings are like a horse unsure of its way
My emotions are endless just like the city
My attitude is just all frizzy
My style is ever changing just like my clothes
My height getting bigger just as my age
There is no going back
I am me, my own person!

Eve Davidson (13)

Freedom

Freedom,
a word thrown about so easily,
unknowing of the world's chaos and calamity.
They say we fight for freedom,
They say we fight for peace,
But it all seems quite contradictory
And the conflict rages on ruthlessly.
Whilst we divide ourselves unnecessarily,
Groups, clans and factions,
But I want you all to know,
segregated we stand vulnerable,
integrated we stand invincible.
Different culture, religion or ethnicity
that we may be, we strive for one thing only.
Without this we can never truly call ourselves humanity.
Freedom.

Rajeshwari Pittala (13)

11 Herbs And Spices

11 delicious herbs and spices
KFC is the very nicest
It cannot be bested
This I have tested
Those 11 tasty herbs and spices.

Andrew Lister (14)

Words

Reading each word,
Picturing the story in your head,
See the words paint a picture,
See the way they are led,
They break your heart or mend your soul,
They crush your dreams or give you hope,
You learn to feel others' pain.
You learn to see life in another way.
You try and try to apply to your own.
You fall in love with the characters,
But between each page you print a piece of your soul
And when it comes to the final page and time to say goodbye
That empty feeling lingers and you realise how quickly the time has passed by.
You try to forget, but it's never the same.
The words have changed you in a way no one can explain.

Jahnavi Thakar (13)

Stalker

A shadow, an empty reflection,
It shares your shape but not your complexion,
A stalker in the light
That hides away at night,
Like a weight you can't get off your back,
Too heavy, big and black.

As the darkness thickens,
The bold appearance sickens,
Fading away
Until it decides to come back out to play.

And when I enter the light again
And the rays shine down and the darkness slain,
Only then will we meet
My stalker with no name,
Who I'll never be able to defeat.

Emma Spence (13)

Pillars Of Bone

I feel like I'm sinking, not fast and painless;
Neither painful nor sudden and unexpected;
But rather slow and in a constant dawning horror,
That of which has been foreseen and expected

But never planned for.

The ground beneath my feet bends with mocking steadiness;
As if completely omnipotent and inevitable in its existence
To its counterpart of which is ascending, stand at the feet of my friends

And the feet of my once-relatable peers.

But now have promoted and have excelled, beyond my reaching hands,
They fade into distant stars,
Pricks of light in a dark world, and of which at the heart

I stay gasping for air.

Frieda Robson (16)

Human

I stand in the midst of darkness and light,
Defeated by the life I live.
I am hopeless and lost,
I am weak and fragile.
I fail to see the beauty that is
Me!
I am a stranger to myself,
I don't know where I am going,
Or where I am.
My heart has been pierced by
The words of those I love.
I am lost because . . .
I am human.

Chengetai Chitemerere (14)
Arundel School, Harare

Overpopulation

'Let there be Man,' Father exclaimed,
Adam and Eve they were then named,
The forbidden fruit they nibbled,
Now their perfect history scribbled.

Spreading far is their offspring now,
Faster than the wind, oh wow,
God's own forests they just devour
And earthly gifts they shall squander.

The more they are, the more danger
That will increase the Lord's anger,
With animals they are killing,
Then on to hot pots, they are cooking.

More and more with education
Can't fill the job application,
From there we get the crooks and thieves,
As many as the old trees' leaves.

With ten kids each from these spouses,
Down go trees to build more houses,
Less oxygen, my lungs so sore,
Soon we'll join the old dinosaur.

More people, more cars and more grease,
Machines, the bad air they release
Into the air, now weather's changed,
Heating the Earth is all we've gained.

To help decrease global warming,
Dwell upon my crucial warning,
As the hot weather seems to spread,
We will cook in Earth's oven, like bread.

So let us rescue our nation
And stop overpopulation.

Lorna Panashe Makuvaro (14)
Arundel School, Harare

I wake up and smile
'Cause it's been a while.
It's been like a whole day
Since I stopped so You could hold me.

I hear the little birds sing
And tears at my sparkling eyes sting.
Lord, You are holy!
My life's Your handwritten story.

Indeed there's none like You,
This for a fact I know is true.
I meditate on Your word every day
Because it helps me in every way.

You made the big sky blue
All glory and praise is unto You.
This may look like just a rhyme
But it's done because of Your love so divine.

Then Easter approaches and I feel guilt
The Lord Jesus Christ's body in three days was rebuilt.
He had to be crucified,
So I could be sanctified.

Thank You Lord for You atoned for my sins,
You were pierced with all those nails and pins.
Dusk is near
And You say, 'Goodnight my dear.'

As I go to sleep
My heart does weep
But I then remember
That sweet dreams I'll endeavour
To have.

Finally I doze
My eyes I contentedly close
And hope to speak to You tomorrow
Because my spirit is cleared of all sorrow

That tomorrow is another day
When I get to say,
'Hey, I'm up, strong and fit,
And I definitely know who did it.'

Ropafadzo Vanessa Manyeza (14)
Arundel School, Harare

My Album Of Memories

From the time I could read
I've kept an album of memories
With my pictures from birth
And even until now
I've gotten to know
Things beyond my imagination

Like, a picture taken
When I was seven
Sitting near a table
Smiling as wide as I was able
Holding a bowl
With a design of an owl

And a black and white picture,
Because of the olden days,
Of my dearly loved grandmas
Posing in a simple way
Sitting on a stack of hay
And not smiling in any way

Special memories must be stored
Just like the fairy tales are told
So that when we are old
We can always glance at our past
And the way years move so fast
Then we can all laugh at last.

Tapiwanashe Mutiracha (14)
Arundel School, Harare

Wisdom

Wisdom
We forever desire it,
But our mindsets are far too enclosed
To cherish our surroundings.
It is appreciating and accepting our neighbours
And neighbours' neighbours' differences.

We tend to want to make people similar to each other,
Assimilation, so we can understand one another.
Hence the world, as chaotic as it is,
Would be without a bother
And absolutely perfect.
But that is utopia,
Which is no place.

We assure ourselves of safety,
We seldom want to take risks because of fear of the unknown.
Opportunities as big as houses
Knock at our doors,
But we brush off our optimistic instincts
And decline offers. We become obliged to one practice
And fertility in the mind is barely happening.

This is why I say we should be wise. It is not rocket science or laborious,
But it is simply accepting one another as we are,
Appreciating, focusing, familiarising,
Being optimistic and taking risks by trying brand new activities.

Wisdom is what it is.
Silence, peace, tranquillity,
It caresses the mind and heart,
And gives us the ability to know no problem is far beyond your boundaries,
As we are built for different purposes with different strengths.
Wisdom.

Mpiwa Gwindi (13)
Arundel School, Harare

Aurora

An aurora borealis
Of emotion.
Finding someone who
Adores you, who thinks you're amazing.
Even with all
Your flaws!

The melting feeling you get
At the sight of them.
The abundant worry at
The sight of their pain.
Now that's love!

Love!
Romance and wedding rings,
Oh la la!
Not only romance
But love, not only
For people, but for the
Things around us and what we do.

I love:
Art, all my emotion is
Expressed through it.
Animals, they are the
Sweetest things that
Make the world go round.
Learning, something that
You will never stop doing.

So love:
An aurora borealis
Of emotion.

Vimbainashe Greatjoy Shava (14)
Arundel School, Harare

Make Way, It's Me!

Everyone has eyes, a nose and a mouth,
So do I, so what makes me stand out?
I'm tall and slender; to me heels aren't crucial,
Skin colour is like toffee, that's not unusual,
Short ebony hair,
Absolutely not rare,
I'm pretty, you're pretty and we're all pretty, right?

But venture into what I call The Me,
A million words describe who I am.
Reserved and generally quiet,
I think before I act,
I'm independent, loving and compassionate,
Respectful, courteous and determined
Open and I don't suppress emotions,
I usually cry it all out.

Words can't bring me down,
I do have faults
But that doesn't mean I'm hopeless,
I'm a diamond; no one can break me,
I take risks,
That's how I know I can accomplish goals.
I'm plucky
And I want to prove I'm 'always' right.

I'm exciting and I lighten the dark, that's certain
By my unexpected remarks, I believe.
I'm rumbustious and loquacious around my friends
My own words are my mirror,
Make way it's me!

Tendai Rutsate (14)
Arundel School, Harare

Just Watch Me Now

You shoved me around
Pushed me to the ground
Never let me be heard
Never let me make a sound

But now I'm free
Free to be me
Just watch me now
I'll make you see

All your snarky comments
That went to my head
Will leave me in peace
And invade you instead

You'll realise soon enough
That I'm different now
I've learnt to fight you
Somewhere, somehow

I'm sure when I say
Just watch me now
I swear you'll be sorry
Just. Watch. Me. Now.

Mudiwa Malaika Mungoshi (13)
Arundel School, Harare

Being Me

I am me.
I believe I can be
All that I want,
All that I dream.

Perfection I seek
Every day, every week.
Disappointment I meet
Sadly.

I try, how I try
To be that kind
Of person everyone
Likes.

But at the same time
I seem to find
I don't care what people
Think.

This life I live
Is a journey to seek
The best me
That I can be.

Sibongile Nyenyedzi Kimberly Kamundimu (13)
Arundel School, Harare

Have You Ever?

Have you ever heard of a life of pain
And one filled with rage?
A life without peace and no one is to blame,
She is given this gift each and every day.

Have you ever been to a place imagined?
A place that holds only shattered dreams,
A place so cold that darkness screams,
A place without hope or comforting dreams,
This is a place I call her soul.

Have you ever heard of a life that crashed suddenly?
One deranged and caged in a series of traumatic events,
A life surrounded by shadows and overwhelmed with shame
She is tired of living this life of heartache and despair.

Have you ever seen a person with so much anguish inside?
A person drowning in sorrow and has no one to revive,
That is the only description left to her name.

So when the tears roll down and no one notices
The only question left will be,
Have you ever?

Mazvita Mupunga (14)
Arundel School, Harare

Theories Of Friendship

I fear it is very wrong of me
And yet I must admit
When someone offers friendship, I want the whole of it
I don't want to share my friends with everybody else
But if I do, I want to be the one special one.

An old friend is better than two new ones
A friendship must be as clear as water
As honest as a mirror
And as firm as rocky mountains.

When two souls destined to become one meet,
They immediately react and a new friendship blossoms
The kind of friend you have
Is a reflection on your feelings and thoughts.

What do I look for in a friend?
I want a crazy friend
Who does not judge nor discourage me
My friend is one who does not care about what others say
All she cares about is our friendship
And so do I.

Tinashe M Mungadzi (14)
Arundel School, Harare

Love

I hit you like a lightning bolt
You never know when I'm going to strike
When you lay your eyes upon the one
You are well and truly on top of the world

I'm like a volcano spewing molten rock
I can't be stopped, I can't be helped
Or like the origin of our world
I can't be explained

In a race I overtake sorrow
And I completely demolish hate
I can force you to do crazy things
I possess your thoughts

So when you do meet the one
Remember me, the lightning bolt
The volcano that cannot be stopped
The champion racer, defeating all.

Laura Henry (13)
Ayr Academy, Ayr

Hate Poem

I am a raging virus that you can't get rid of.
Every time you see them playing, I get to work.
You felt me when he pushed you to the floor,
I heard you saying, 'I want to bang his head off the door!'
When your mum said no I started to flow.
First I go to your feet, they heat up,
Then rise through your legs, they wobble,
Then your brain . . .
That's when all that happened,
His head hit the door, their bodies hit the floor
And your mum, well that was just gore.

James Cooper (12)
Ayr Academy, Ayr

Gone

They're gone.
All of them, just gone from my life.
I'm crushed.
I'm scared, I don't know what to do.
Everything I knew before is gone.
I can't believe it.
I'm in the dark.
No one will tell me why.

I can't live like this.
I need to live.
I can't be . . . this.
I'm dreaming, I'll pinch myself
And wake up.

But I can't.
I'm helpless. I'm nothing.
They're not gone.
I am.
I am deep in the ground, or in a furnace burning.
I cannot stop it.

It hurts so badly.
I hate it.
I cannot stop myself from being scattered.
I cannot stop myself from moving.
At home, my friends move on.
So do I, but not in that way
Because I'm gone.

Emma Eales
Beeslack High School, Penicuik

The Treasure Tree

Pushing through bitter winds
Face bent looking, my boots
Creaked through snow-filled fields
The land dappled like a white wave.

Then I saw you, bent in shame
Your arm lying twisted and torn.
Oh wistfulness, time has stolen fame
Many a harder battle you've worn.

You used to tower above me
A mighty warrior at his peak.
I was so wrong. The mist has cleared
It is I who rises higher.

Five hundred winters you stood, dominant.
I used to jump and climb and wondered
How tall you were, how powerful.
Now I am higher, it's not all I thought it would be.

Hew Murray (13)
Beeslack High School, Penicuik

Perfection

Flowers sleep through a breeze
Crickets sing in the trees
The moon in the sky
Glows sparkling bright
Indulging the world
in a sleepy night.

Heather Quinn (13)
Beeslack High School, Penicuik

Happy Meal

The girl was limping to the town
The stab wound too deep to manage
The clown surprisingly brutal
The laugh so soulless
Eyes so blood-hungry.
Kicks her down
In a pool of blood.
Only silent weeping can be heard.
He crouched down and whispered in that cold voice,
'That's what you get for stealing my nose.'
Only darkness . . .
Only darkness.

Jamie Keith
Beeslack High School, Penicuik

Perfect Harmony

The sound of your voice is music
To my ears
The steady strum of the guitars and my heartbeat fit perfectly together,
In time,
As one,
With your music.

Constantly overwhelmed at your voices,
Appreciating every high and low note
The softness making my skin tingle as your voices merge with the ongoing melody
I'm singing,
Smiling,
With your music.

Your voices mingle with the loud clashes and beats of the drum
Creating a river of happiness which surges through me
I appreciate you,
Every day,
And your music.

Maya George
Blanchelande College, Guernsey

Pollution Is A Dragon

Pollution is a dragon,
Its venomous smoke fills the air,
In the wake of its destruction,
It grins mischievously because it doesn't care,
But knows it's caused an eruption.

Pollution is a dragon,
His enormous body wrecks the forest,
Crushing down all the trees,
He thinks it's funny to be honest,
But knows nobody agrees.

Pollution is a dragon,
Its catastrophic claws create chaos,
Scraping and scratching the beautiful city,
He rather enjoys the people's loss,
Although, he knows it's not pretty.

Pollution is a dragon,
His sharp, spiky teeth are going to cause extinction,
Gobbling and munching on defenceless prey,
He couldn't care less for affection.
Is the end of the world on its way?

Pollution is a dragon,
He's had his fun,
But it has begun,
To disappear.
Like the old, wonderful world has
Year by year.

But now he wonders why
He made people cry,
And animals die.
Was it really worth it?

William Owens (11)
Castell Alun High School, Flintshire

Whatever That Means

I look at my school -
Obviously full of children.
The trend is to be cool -
Whatever that means.

I look at my class.
'Obviously' to be liked,
You have to have 'sass' -
Whatever that means.

I look at the others -
'Obviously' they all have 'swagger' -
Whatever that means.

Then I look at myself -
A lonely, anti-social freak.
No 'selfies' of myself.
I'm a dork -
Whatever that means.

Nobody understands me -
Well my family does a bit.
But the way I see things,
The way I think,
My friends don't get a bit.

The loneliness and the anger
Is sometimes too much.
The anger spurts out of me,
As wild as chicks in a clutch.

All I need is someone to hold
And someone to hold me.
Because I don't have a 'bay' -
Whatever that means.

Joshua Berdouk (11)
Castell Alun High School, Flintshire

Don't Sulk

Don't sulk
Even when the bulk
Of worrying doom,
Sits out there, in the gloom,
Because . . .

Happiness is like the light
It never gives you woe,
It reaches up to its full height,
Showing off all its full might.
But what is like the light so bright?
The answer is the snow.

Happiness is like the cotton,
When near, you never think of slaughter.
The white fluffy cloud, never forgotten,
No matter how dirty, it will never look rotten.
But what will never be rock-bottom?
The answer is the water.

Happiness is like the sun
Giving off its full righteousness,
Making you want to run,
Faster and faster, just playing dumb.
But what is the thing that makes all the fun?
The answer is . . .

Happiness!

Ffion Smith (11)
Castell Alun High School, Flintshire

Oh Sweet Esme

Oh Esme, my sweet Esme,
How you've changed my world, entering my life.
If you were a human, you'd be my wife.
Oh Esme, my sweet Esme,
Every pet should have a nature like yours,
So sweet, so soft and such cute little paws.
Oh Esme, my sweet Esme,
Every hamster should have your special heart,
When you want to, you can move like a dart.
Oh Esme, my sweet Esme,
Your fur is luxury velvet to stroke,
You're so special, you're simply bespoke.
Oh Esme, my sweet Esme,
You're black and white, just like a Dalmatian,
I thank the Lord for your whole creation.
Oh Esme, my sweet Esme,
Your ears are like saucers, your eyes black beads,
I love you so much my heart swells with need.
Oh Esme, my sweet, sweet Esme.

Ella Bradley (11)
Castell Alun High School, Flintshire

My Own Worlds

I fought for what was right and found my inner self with Tris,
Made tough decisions and protected loved ones with Katniss.

I fought back and survived with Hazel Grace.
I knew I'd found a new friend when I read that first page.

My life is like a book and I am the author,
I know this book will never be read by another.

I was the chosen one with Harry, I stuck with him until the very end.
I know that Hermione is probably my best friend.

My life is like a book and I am the author,
I know this book will never be read by another.

I loved and cared with Bella Swan.
Had adventures with Bilbo, they were so much fun.

My life is like a book and I am the author,
I know this book will never be read by another.

Grace Davies (11)
Castell Alun High School, Flintshire

The Worries Of War

The first worry of war,
Is the sight of guts and gore.
Please, the macabre no more.
Why can't we turn around
And close this harrowing door on war?

The second worry of war,
Is the feeling of endless sore.
Please, the plague no more.
Why can't we turn around
And close this harrowing door on war?

The final worry of war,
Is the endless knowing of the poor.
Please, the deprivation no more.
Why can't we turn around
And close this harrowing door on war?

Cerys Jones (11)
Castell Alun High School, Flintshire

Friendship

Friendship is my shield and armour
Protecting me from bad things and people.
My life is like a battle and drama.
My life is a mess but you make me happy.

When I fall you are there to help me rise.
You make me stronger and invincible.
When I'm sad you give me a nice surprise.
When I'm down you help me rise to the top.

We have our ups and downs but we stay friends.
You help me grow in life and to stay strong.
Our bond will never end until the end.
We will be best friends until the end of time.

Nicky Wong Rush (12)
Castell Alun High School, Flintshire

Fairy

Wings sparkling above the clearing,
Bursting with vibrant colours,
Weaving past tall sunflowers,
Entering the pearl clouds.

Shining eyes captured a tiny bunch
Of gorgeous fuchsias,
Peeking out from the glistening leaves
Of a cherry tree.

Fluttering down to the blooming buds,
Taking the stems in her delicate palms,
She plucked the flowers from their roots,
Sweetness filled the wispy air.

Shooting up to the top of the cherry tree
Surrounded by huge leaves,
She perched upon a dainty branch
And slipped a flower in her smooth hair.

Holding the others forwards,
Young hands clasped them,
A baby resting in a cot,
Made of soft leaves and grass.

She leaned over the smiling soul
And took it in her arms,
Planting a kiss on its blonde curly hair,
The child's laughs and giggles surrounded her.

Aurora Hampson (14)
City Of Norwich School, Norwich

Alone And Hopeless

Teary raindrops crawl down
The splintered windows rotted with age,
Like forgotten promises
And broken dreams.

The dull, gloomy sea lashes out,
Against the frozen shore,
As if desperate for
Someone to hear it.

Bottles with grimy, splintered glass
Are lined up solemnly, waiting in vain
For somebody to come,
To drink the sadness out of them.

Buildings all around the solitary street
Hunch into the shadows.
Echoes of haunting memories
Bounce off the walls, left to die.

The city, left alone.
Alone and hopeless.
It stares, isolated, at the horizon,
Awaiting its end that will never come.

Lily Pierce (11)
City Of Norwich School, Norwich

Lost Love

Not a rose or a kiss but something forever kept
A scar you can't see. A heart smashed to smithereens

Ten thousand memories never forgotten
No hope in return
Only loss hovers in the air
The love lost forever.

Amie Ramsdale (12)
City Of Norwich School, Norwich

Angry Spirits

Merry men laughing and joyous,
Wake up a fire,
Launching the drinks like rockets,
The world went up in fire.

An empty sky as cold as biting ice,
Smoke from the pub wanders up to pollute,
Birds run towards the empty grey sky,
Clouds take detours around the sadness.

Sitting in a field,
Once filled with corn and crying crows,
Nowadays only a ragged scarecrow occupies it,
It's blackened and twisted into nothingness.

The house I grew up in is burnt to its feet,
Upstairs rooms walk downstairs to weep.
School where I spent hour after hour learning,
Is gone, it ran away with time.

An empty world smothered in neglect,
Once beautiful and full of laughter and play,
Now ugly and full of angry spirits,
Staring at my world, I am drinking sadness.

Holly Maw (11)
City Of Norwich School, Norwich

The Rain Will Fall

As cold as a dragon's unloved heart the hail splinters down
Over the edge of the world the powdery clouds fly like wishes
Of fairies that never lived
In distant lands the sun shines as bright as the Earth's core
In the stories of the ancient people, elves' feet patter on the path like rain.

Catey Clancy (12)
City Of Norwich School, Norwich

Things Found In A Shadow's Pocket

A face that no one's seen
Keys to unlock his anger

His never-ending chains
His sight

The life he will never have
The measured weep of his painful cry

The thought of being real
His slow cold breath

The slow skip he stole from a girl
The scars he gets from when they walk

A pocket-sized chest where he keeps his happiness
Unopened

The nightmares that he treasured
His heart that he abandoned years ago

The wish of life.

Jessica Balls (11)
City Of Norwich School, Norwich

Items Found In A Shadow's Pocket

A cauldron of atmosphere,
A case of terror,
A haunting stare,
A packet of tissues to fill with distress,
A nightmare of anxiety,
A sinful novel of horror,
The emotions of a scared young boy.

Ruby Ashby-Otun (12)
City Of Norwich School, Norwich

Piano

Reluctant to make beautiful music,
It was still able.
The black and white masterpiece standing,
All pride lost.
Unknowingly gorgeous.
A decade of sweet music
Gone.
No longer flowing like a stream
But stumbling over roots.

The roots
That numb you
Down.

Down
Through a soul.
Down
Through a skeleton.
Down
To nothing.

Sophie Wyatt (13)
City Of Norwich School, Norwich

My City Is Burnt

My city is burnt,
Not a single brick left standing.

It all started this morning when I was having my daily coffee,
I peered through the dusted windows, devastation was written bold and clear,
I could see thick grey smoke billowing into the sky,
Once blue now covered by a veil of darkness.
Crimson flames sneaking from house to house.

Fire!

I felt my heart in my throat,
My breathing uneven,
It was raining ash,
The floor was painted in debris.

Chaos was snaking its way through the villages.

Grace Erlam (13)
City Of Norwich School, Norwich

Four Seasons Haiku

Pearl-white snow shining,
Below the sharp, bright sunlight,
A thousand diamonds.

Now spring comes along,
Flowers blooming in the warmth,
May comes to an end.

In the fields of gold,
Sunflowers bright as a star,
Glisten in the heat.

Falling from the trees,
Are the golden leaves of God,
Everlastingly.

Ethan Sallis (12)
City Of Norwich School, Norwich

Mixed Emotions

I walk along the street,
Smiling at everyone I meet.

Like a dog walking alone,
No friends and no bone.

Sun shining so
Bright through the trees.

I'm hungry so,
I beg on my knees.

Happy families,
Going in and out of their homes.

And I'm on the street,
Bored and alone.

Millie Milner (11)
City Of Norwich School, Norwich

Deprivation

Drinking sadness,
An elixir so sweet.
With this terrible life,
Melancholy is hard to beat.

Consuming sadness,
A form of looming deprivation.
Made to conform,
To the constraints of this generation.

Violent sadness,
The wait for an agonising death.
Life flashing past your eyes,
As you draw in a final breath.

Sky Barwood (13)
City Of Norwich School, Norwich

Untitled

The last breath of a mythical creature, never seen, and never will be.
The lick of the lips of a tiger, hunting its prey.
The aftermath of a giant falling to death, not an earthquake, but a wisp of air.
Breeze.

The zap of a miniature wasp, not even a microscope can detect,
Thousands of them, but it doesn't hurt.
The tear of a decrepit god, hit by Zeus' rage in the sky.
Raindrops.

The dust left behind of a million horses gone to battle, mixed up,
Twisted up, sucking everything in its path.
Anger, anger, anger it chants as it sweeps through swiftly.
Hurricane.

Daria George (12)
City Of Norwich School, Norwich

Life And Death

A bird, with a broken wing.
An abandoned house, on a rundown road.
A forgotten ghost floating in the harsh wind.
A wedding ring, unused and unloved.
A train station, never seen the happiness of children.
A pub where no one has ever drunk.
A school full of dirty, diseased rats.

A foot with purple bruises.
Old bread full of live maggots.
An empty chest but filled with lies, suffering and torment.
A cracked glass window, never cleaned.
A dead goat, blood spewing all over the cold floor.

Hayden Perry (12)
City Of Norwich School, Norwich

An Empty Glass

I used to drink a glass of beer, then the winds changed
and in the air you smell the bitterness of war
and in your ears you hear the cries of men who gave their lives.

The fields of war are covered in bodies,
where once children played that is no more,
the happy laughter turns into disaster,
the silence is broken with bangs and shots.

Now the glass is half empty, and the strong men turn weak,
the houses sink in and the place is deserted.

The glass is now empty, there is nothing to win
and all I am doing is drinking sadness.

Andries Quinton (12)
City Of Norwich School, Norwich

Emptiness

As I walk down a lonely road,
I hear the sobbing of children and the hungry wailing of the birds.
The emptiness of the lane creates
my sorrowfull future fate.

The depressing feeling that my hopes may never come true.
I sat under a burnt out lamp post.

I saw ghostly figures as I sat trembling in fear,
Swirling all around me and creating a light mist,
I could not see anything.
I opened my eyes and everything was just how it was.
Empty.

Joseph Baxter (12)
City Of Norwich School, Norwich

Remembrance

A small hopeful flower in a field of loss
The only sign of hope after a clash of death,
The little red petals unfolding the hope and remembrance
Onto a field of sorrow.

An old tree scarred by death
Stripped of its glorious cloak of leaves and bark
Whimpering there in the field of remembrance.

Fields of health and colours torn apart by the monstrous war,
Looted of its colours, burnt of its health, now just a field of mines.

All the signs of war are a mile away but the remembrance lives on.

Nathanael Ward (11)
City Of Norwich School, Norwich

Endings

Everything has an end,
hunger, happiness and life,
they are all spinning,
twisting and turning is easy.

Some wait for an end,
some receive,
others time is taken from them,
unwillingly drawn,
but an end always comes,
unwelcome, uninvited,
you don't know when or how,
an end will come.

Kathleen West
Clydeview Academy, Gourock

Demons

'Go away,' I tell them,
But they never listen,
They stay,
Forever,
Never going,
Never ever leaving.

Nobody listens,
They brush me away,
Thinking I'm mad,
But I know who's there,
I know
And I always will.

I try to fight them,
I really do,
But still they carry on,
Tormenting me,
Laughing at me,
Willing me to try again.

I don't know,
I don't think I ever will,
I will be forever stuck,
In a turning spasm,
Of laughing and cackling.

Who knows what they are?
Who?
Tell me,
But I call them demons,
What do you call them?
Because only you know.

Georgia Virtue (12)
Earlston High School, Earlston

Ants

We have a miserable life,
Sent to work until we die,
So that others may do the same.
We crowd round the tower.
Our cutters have
Prepared us our heavy loads.
Three times our size and weight
They truly are a hefty burden.
Yet we must carry them forever
Till we reach our destination
While we deposit our cargo and trudge back
To start again.
We never sleep
Till one day we collapse into oblivion
At the end of a miserable life.
We are the sad ones.
We are the slaves.

Hannah Marion Jones (13)
Earlston High School, Earlston

Overrated

Everything is overrated.
Nutella is overrated,
Selfie sticks are overrated,
Football is overrated,
Boy bands with stupid haircuts are overrated,
Even writing poems about everything being overrated is overrated!

Everything.

But we let it. We let ourselves and everything else because we want to fit in
And even when you try to stand out it's because you want to fit in.
So try to be underrated for a day, month or year or don't
Because that would be trying and trying is overrated.
No matter what you do or who you try to be in this world that's all you'll ever be.

Overrated.

Cassidy McGairy (13)
Eastbank Academy, Glasgow

The Things We Do

He'd let the fire that courses through his veins consume him,
Before he'd let harm come to her.

He'd give up his memories
Before he would see his friend heartbroken again.

She'd sooner die that let her father, the man who destroyed her family,
Destroy it again.

He'd rather suffer his own pain
Than see the girl he won't admit he loves upset.

She'd drug herself unconscious
Before she let her daughter remember what she gave up her whole life to forget.

But I guess that's just the things we do.

Kayleigh Neil
Eastbank Academy, Glasgow

Beatrix Potter's Little Friends

Peter, Peter, what are you doing
In Mr McGregor's garden?
Rabbit, Rabbit, what's that you're chewing?
You'd better beg his pardon.

Squirrel, Squirrel, sing a silly riddle,
To annoy the old Owl Brown.
Nutkin, Nutkin, better watch your tail,
You've made Owl Brown frown.

Benjamin, Benjamin, you're a cheeky little bunny,
Who got trapped in a basket with Peter.
Bunny, Bunny, your story's very funny,
Trapped by a cat – did you meet her?

Mrs, Mrs, washing your clothes,
Get them nice and clean.
Tiggy-Winkle, wrinkle your nose,
No dirty marks to be seen.

Jemima, Jemima, never trust a fox
Who takes you to tumble-down shed.
Puddle-Duck, it was all a hoax,
Thanks to puppies that took you home to bed.

Flopsy, Flopsy, in trouble once more
And been tied up in a sack.
Bunnies, bunnies, the wee mouse tore
A hole so you could all run back.

Jeremy, Jeremy, off to catch some minnows,
Whilst fishing from your lily pad.
Fisher, Fisher, swallowed by a trout,
But your Macintosh made him mad.

Abigail Watson (12)
Eastwood High School, Glasgow

Nuclear Bombs

What's the end that humans will find?
It could be caused by our own kind,
Person to person, friend to friend,
Nuclear bombs could cause the end.

People starve and need some money,
It's used for bombs, that's not funny,
Basically they're war that you can send,
Nuclear bombs could cause the end.

It is all caused by mankind's fights,
Weapons that can snuff out all lights,
Now enemy, used to be a friend,
Nuclear bombs could cause the end.

People will starve, people will thirst,
People will drown, decide the worst,
It's all over when someone presses 'send',
Nuclear bombs could cause the end.

Jamie Newbigging (13)
Gleniffer High School, Paisley

Ode To A Chicken

Oh chicken,
You are so sweet,
You are my favourite kind of meat.
You come from a farm where the farmers are nice,
You can be eaten with bread or rice.
Oh chicken,
You are so tasty,
I even have you with some gravy.
I can't believe you taste so good,
Oh chicken,
You are my favourite food.

Harry Carlin (13)
Gleniffer High School, Paisley

Corpus Ex Machina

Fires my furnace
To make me fly
To shatter the stars
And to spilt the sky

Knuckles clench
No reason why I
Should hold back
All of them just need to die

My motor running
Ready to roll
Cuts, blood and bruises
Don't take a toll

Teeth grinding
Spinning the gears
Turning the engine
Fighting the tears

Pistons fire
Forcing blood and fuel
Controlling emotion
There's only one rule

Body's a machine
Built to survive
All the others
They just stand by

Beat them to the ground
Laugh as they cry
I've put up for so long
With all the pain and the lies

Stand alone
I'm not afraid
All the others are weak
Addicted to praise

To being liked
To being loved
Let go of it all
No one looks down from above

I'll follow you home
I'll break your bones
Hit me again
I like the pain

Violence and life
It's all a game
It'll come to an end
No matter what we do

So what's to stop me
From playing with you?

Punches and kicks
Encourage me more
Pull you to the ground
Hit your face off the floor

Again and again

My motor's still running
Chains turn, girders crack
Doesn't matter
No holding me back

Hating you
It's like a drug to me
Without that drug
I don't know what I'd be

Just another machine
Ticking day to day
Till my motor stops running
And I fade away.

Struan McCorrisken (16)
Gleniffer High School, Paisley

Winter

Winter's in the middle of autumn and spring
When it arrives I'm so happy it makes me want to sing
Christmas and snow and a huge holiday
I want to cheer it and thank it, hip hip hooray!

Something about the cold makes me want to jump around
Untouched snow, how it looks perfect on the ground
Hot chocolate and blankets on cold winter nights
Everybody's happy, there aren't any fights!

At this time of year kids are being good
For Santa to visit their neighbourhood.
Bringing presents and sweeties and happiness too
Santa brings joy wherever he goes, that's true!

Once winter has gone, and the snow has all melted,
The sun has come out and spring's where we're headed.
I find myself dreaming about winter
And thoughts of snow and excitement linger.

Gemma Williams (13)
Gleniffer High School, Paisley

Chocolate

Oh chocolate I love you, oh chocolate I do.
You turn me around whenever I'm down.
You're very nutritious and extremely delicious.
You come in white, dark and milk
And you're like the finest silk.
My favourite is white, but the others are still nice.
Oh chocolate I love you, oh chocolate I do.

Scott Glassford (13)
Gleniffer High School, Paisley

A Soldier's Mind

Seeking the enemy's danger zones
Listening to their loud carbon drones
Thinking of his family and needing to yearn
He knows, it won't be long until he shall return

His love's commitments to his fatal career
How she struggles to hold back a tear
And how all her thoughts rapidly churn
She knows, it won't be long until he shall return

As his melancholy days, by him they drag
His country, with pride, they fly their flag
His family and love, in desire their heart's burn
They know, it won't be long until he shall return

The cramped letters he sends
To make his family's worries end
Now he has had his turn
He knows, it is now he shall return.

Rachel Ward (13)
Gleniffer High School, Paisley

The Beach – Haiku

The waves are so high
My ice cream melts in my hands
Oh, I love the beach.

Lewis Logan (13)
Gleniffer High School, Paisley

Chocolate Heaven

Cocoa beans – tastiest ever invention
The pleasures they bring are too many to mention
Plain, milky, dark and white
With strawberries and marshmallows what a delight.

Fountains, sauces, sprinkles and dips
Just the thought has me licking my lips
Heavenly, divine and sickly sweet
Velvety, smooth my favourite treat.

Galaxy, Milky Bar, Twirl and Twix
How I live for my daily chocolate fix
So many to choose from, where do I start?
Chocolate's most definitely the way to my heart.

Gemma Lamont (13)
Gleniffer High School, Paisley

Teenagers – Haiku

Teenagers confused
About friends and family
Smile and laugh, it helps.

Abby Gibson (13)
Gleniffer High School, Paisley

The Depth Of Love

Happiness is a thing with no limit;
It reaches as high as clouds and higher,
But love must be worked for.
You must try hard.

To love someone is to give them your heart,
But that makes it so much easier to break.
Some brush off heartbreak,
But it wasn't true love if it was that easy;
Others dwell on the past.

You can be as in love as the stars that shine,
But without trust it means nothing.
Love is a cruel thing;
It leaves you as broken as a bottle on the beach.
Some say only a fool will fall in love,
But I disagree.

Soulmates and love at first sight are the things of dreams;
But you may believe in them.
You may have seen your one true love before;
Down the street or across town.

Your other half may live in a different country – speak a different language.
But love is love,
No matter what shape or size.
So say what you like;
It won't matter to me.
I only believe what I want to believe.

Rowan Ferguson (14)
Grangemouth High School, Grangemouth

A Life

A life:
Full of mysteries,
Full of accomplishments,
Full of sadness.
First, passing from door to door,
Never knowing what is coming.
Second, finding glory,
That by the end, has little meaning.
Third, your favourite thing about life,
Slowly crawling into your mind,
But could be put to a stop by the fear inside you:
Waking up at any moment,
Every single part of it,
At its best,
Passing by with a *snap!*
And even when time has let you down,
Or when anxiety is at its worst,
You have to think,
Time is of the essence!
So don't get down,
Don't waste it,
Don't worry,
And be happy.
Have fun,
It will pay off.
In a not so distant future,
You will find your favourite thing from when you struggled,
In a picture.
Before, trying to find its pair,
Now living a happy life with its pair, never having any troubles again.
A life:
Full of mysteries,
Full of accomplishments,
Full of sadness.

Marie Leggett-Vasilieva (12)
International School of Prague, Prague

Blue

Blue is the feeling of a Gatorade sloshing around in your stomach.
Blue is the feeling of guilt and sadness.
Blue is the colour of a short, dark December day.
Blue is the scary sight of meeting a shark in the deep ocean.
Blue is the taste of cheap candy that leaves your tongue coloured.
Blue is the thought of drowning right as you are about to reach the surface.
Blue is the tough of a cold toilet seat.
Blue is the image of a frozen pond in the middle of nowhere.
Blue is the experience of not being able to breathe.
Blue is the warning of a coming storm.
Blue is the sign of the unforgiving cold.
Blue is the feeling of cold wind on your neck.
Blue is the taste of a cold, hard pizza.
Blue is the scare of a horror movie.
Blue is the horrific feeling of having a bee land on your body.
Blue is the annoying realisation that your laptop is out of charge.
Blue is the sound of bad news.
Blue is the sight of a failed test.
Blue is the loud pop of a balloon.
Blue is the disappointment of finding a flat basketball.
Blue is the sight of an empty toilet paper roll right when you need it.
Blue is the Fantastic Four.
Blue is the taste of cold chocolate milk.
Blue is the touch of chewing gum on the underside of a desk.
Blue is the feeling of no Internet connection.
Blue is the sight of a broken iPhone.
Blue is the reminder that you have no clean socks for tomorrow.
Blue is the swallow of dinner without tasting any of it.
Blue is the rejection of a high five.
Blue is the stuck of bubblegum to your backside
And blue is a colour that is untrustworthy and scary.
When there is a hole in my heart, blue comes to mind.
It is the way I feel without you, completely blind.

Darman Bacha (13)
International School of Prague, Prague

To All With A Unique Glance

We can't choose everything
We can't keep expecting
We have to learn to live
A life that won't cause anguish

We all live different lives
We were never all allies
We turned each other down
Turned smiles into frowns

We learned to hate difference
We judged people on appearance
We made people's lives a terror
Making them become an error

We thought appearance really mattered
We never cared about the lives we shattered
We never thought to give a chance
To the ones who differ from our glance

So I ask you today
To put all thoughts away
To give a chance
To those with a different glance

We should all look beyond what we can see
And find something on which we agree
We can all live in a world full of love
If we define ourselves all as one.

Tereza Bártová (13)
International School of Prague, Prague

Look Up Little Girl

Look up little girl
And break that glass.
Look up little girl
And make your light last.
Take my hand little girl,
Grow strong and tall.
Don't hold back little girl
And you will not fall.
While you are as dainty as the rose
And as beautiful as a sunrise.
You are as fast as a cheetah
And as strong as the river.
Show your mind little girl
And you will be known.
Go on and try little girl
And you will show that you are not owned.
While you are as dainty as the rose
And as beautiful as a sunrise.
You are as fast as a cheetah
And as strong as the river.
So look up little girl
And make right in our world.

Emma Neuman (11)
International School of Prague, Prague

I Am The Girl In The Shadows

I am the girl in the shadows, the one nobody sees.

Every week day I go through the door, looks like a cobra opening its jaw,
eating everyone, especially me.

I am the girl in the shadows, the one nobody sees.

Recess is not a break, no, not for me,
it is a time for me to hide and not get seen.

I am the girl in the shadows, the one nobody sees.

I see everyone in their groups and their gangs,
laughing at jokes, having a great time,
having someone to catch you when you fall.
I wish I was one of them.

I am the girl in the shadows, the one nobody sees.
I am the girl in the shadows, the one nobody sees.

I get beaten, I fall down
I can't get up,
I can't get up,
no one cares to see.

I am the girl in the shadows, the one nobody sees.
I wish one day they will see the real me.

Nicole O'Mara (11)
International School of Prague, Prague

When I Was Your Age . . .

When I was your age we liked different things.
We played outside in nature, at night we sat next to the fire.
In the morning we looked at dew and thought of life.
We could sit and look at the small and exciting life of ants.
We could wait from sunrise to sunset.
When I was your age we liked different things.

Brailovskiy Arseniy (12)
International School of Prague, Prague

Going In Circles

As a dream I once had
It repeats itself over and over
a ghost half dead chasing me,
trying to kill me, trying to eat me.

Could you kill a ghost
by stabbing its heart with a stone
and throwing her into the river?
Or is it just a fairy tale of how to get
yourself killed?

Or is it by running up a tower
as a tour guide,
or by how far you run away
in a deep, dark forest?

Or is it by becoming so old that
the deathbed seems safe by itself?
Or by the way you try attacking the ghost
only to end up half alive yourself?

Maybe it's by a way that no one knows
or maybe by the way that you must . . .

Face your fears and believe you are not alone.

Lillian Therese Pinard (12)
International School of Prague, Prague

All It Takes

All it takes is a light blue sea and a little wind,
All it takes is a dead battery and the dark starts caving in,
All it takes is a little rain and the floods are everywhere,
All it takes is something you see and I swear you'll run for there.

Emma Arden Farmer (12)
International School of Prague, Prague

The Performance

My palms are sweating,
my knees shaking,
I am scared.
I see the dim light on the stage,
I see my parents seated amongst the audience,
'Get ready!' whispers my teacher.
She pats my tutu, and as I hear my name
pushes me out there.
Music blares out of the speaker,
but I just stand there,
terrified,
people gasp
and tears start to well up in my eyes,
I stand up straight
and just tell myself to toughen up,
I weakly get into my starting position,
I feel my sweat, smudging my swan make-up,
I close my eyes, and tell myself I can do this,
I look at my teacher and nod,
the music starts again,
only this time
I dance.

Sophia Hausknecht (13)
International School of Prague, Prague

Quad

The high-pitch whine hits me
I am standing here ready
I grab the remote sticks
It is sitting there with the blades spinning
The wind is pushing away the grass
As I start to ascend I watch carefully
First up down
Then from side to side
I'm confident now
I start to fly it round
Faster and faster
And then I hear it
A loud and clear
Beeeep
This is what I dread
The battery is almost dead
I start to come in for the landing
I cut the engines just as it touches the ground
I pick it up and turn it off
I plug it in to charge
Ready for tomorrow
When I shall fly again.

Milan Rasche (13)
International School of Prague, Prague

So It Happened

I've tried to dunk all my life,
If I could make it, it could change my life.
Jumping up, falling, I might just stop playing,
But one day, I had a dream,
A dream that I touched the net.
'Mom, I touched the net!' I screamed.
I wanna fly! I wanna fly like MJ, I thought.
Pumped. I got up. Ready for the day. I put on my clothes.

I put my Js on my feet.
Went outside. Looked up at the basket.
I warmed up, and I pumped myself up to the max, I was ready to triumph.
Jump to the maximum height.
I faced the basket ready to start.

I ran up to it, and finally I jumped,
It seemed like I was flying, I got so high,
So incredibly high and dunked.

The commentator said, 'Oh what a dunk,'
Then I realised I had no luck.
It wasn't possible to happen in real life
So it happened in NBA 2K15.

Albert Velikonja (11)
International School of Prague, Prague

Nothing

Nothing . . . nothing, nothing, nothing
My brain is empty
After three hours of testing
My brain is flat with only
The little waves on the sand in the deep dry Sahara desert
The sun scorching everything I am trying to think of
Can't wait to leave and lay on my bed.

Stan Loomans (12)
International School of Prague, Prague

A World

A world of war,
A world of peace,
A world where no one gets to eat.
A world of poor,
A world of rich,
A world where no one gets to drink.
A world of old,
A world of young,
A world where no one wants to live.
A world of sad,
A world of joy,
A world where everyone feels the pain.
Why must it be this way?
Why must we fight?
Why can't we desperately see the light?
I don't want this world,
I don't want this life,
I don't want to have to draw the knife.
Feed the children.
Give them water.
Save the future.

Viviana Lanzarotti (13)
International School of Prague, Prague

Loneliness

Hot sun crawling down quietly
like a piece of shiny gold
in the huge, peaceful sea.

Dried mountain
got a crack
of his fierce mind.
He had a fierce mind of loneliness
so strong that it got a crack.

Boiling, deep breath of wind
coming down from the huge, giant mountain.

Sand travelled
with wind together gently.

Then sand was really annoyed
that the wind had left her alone
in the huge, lonely world.

Rude, dried sand hugged water,
forcing them to be quiet.

Then the loneliness happens again.

Yeajin Han (12)
International School of Prague, Prague

Invisible

I wave my hand
But no one replies
I walk right to them
My life is a lie
No one can see me
No one can hear me
I'm just a ghost
That's what irritates me the most.

Mia Romem (13)
International School of Prague, Prague

My Friend

My feet fall into the endless ground,
Like a person is drowned.
My tongue is eaten by bits of salty creatures,
I can hear the yell of the teachers,
My hand forms a piece of art,
Making me look smart,
The crowds go loud
Like horses in the wild,
It is closer to the gateway,
Just make it go straightaway,
The blob of black
Has to make flack,
To the enemy's side,
Is like an endless ride,
It's full of danger and harm,
But it is a charm,
I don't quit,
That's why I like it,
It's my friend,
Beach volleyball.

Tereza Zakova (13)
International School of Prague, Prague

You Need To Breathe Air

Friends,
Friends that love you,
Friends that care,
The ones that help you breathe air,
As simple as that they help you through life,
Friends that help you anywhere,
Whether you are together or apart,
Where we will always remain is in each other's hearts.

Nina Burghouts (12)
International School of Prague, Prague

Icy Power

A hard ground covers twenty-nine percent of the Earth's surface,
Upon that ground bare trees and long grass protrude.
A silky white blanket reverses its purpose and cools the world with its icy power.

Grey clouds part to reveal a brightly burning sun,
Light erupts from a volcano in the sky,
The quilt of snow transforms from a cold powder to a slushy soup of dead plants and water,

Overgrown grass and weeds reappear in the muddy soil,
Leaves grow to dress the branches of trees and bushes,
Birdsong rings out in the clean morning air,
Spring.
The season which turns the lifeless winter into a time of beauty and joy,
Eight months later,
A chilly breeze will sweep over one side of the planet,
And the patterns of the year will continue like they always have,
And will for a long time to come.

Mary Grace Cook (12)
International School of Prague, Prague

Football

You kick the ball and hope to get it in the goal,
You see the ball fly as it hits the pole,
The ball is at your feet,
The pressure is all on you,
As you stare at your fabulous shoe,
I see the defender coming with his superflys,
As I stare right into his eyes,
Fakes left, goes right,
As he passes my sight,
He goes past one, he goes past two,
Oh watch out, he's coming past you.

Alex Pildes (13)
International School of Prague, Prague

Running Tears

I told you my story,
I told you my fears,
I told you I had been left before,
But you didn't listen.

You took away my hope,
You told me lies.
I gave you my trust,
But you left me alone.

You hurt my feelings,
You broke my heart.
I let you hold my hand,
But you denied me.

I told you I liked you,
I told you I loved you.
I gave you my time,
But you left me for another.

Lea Kjaer (13)
International School of Prague, Prague

The Key

The key to my heart is when I see people laughing
Being happy
The key to my heart is your heart
Your art
The key to my heart is the key
Finding it
The key to my heart is the push
The twist
The key to my heart is the opening
You opened my heart
And closed it.

Anezka Liskova (11)
International School of Prague, Prague

Not My Birthday

Lipno is a cake.
The mountain made of chocolate
And snow like icing.

The hotel is a
Gingerbread house on a plate
Frosted so smoothly.

Skiers cut the snow
Like a birthday cake for kids
With thin, straight, sharp skis.

I have only one.
On it is a chair for me.
'Hi Roo!' yell my friends.

My face is red like
A cherry on top of the
cake. Don't look at me.

Roo Wiener (12)
International School of Prague, Prague

Homework

I leave my homework until the last minute,
Never doing it quite well.
I get in trouble with the teachers,
Causing everyone to yell.
While I laugh at what is happening,
I may not understand.
Homework may be good for me,
It's giving a helping hand.
It's like a step that helps me achieve,
What I want in school.
I guess I should be pleased 'bout it,
'Cause I don't want to be a fool.

Elly Simon (13)
International School of Prague, Prague

Dream Box

I put all my dreams in a box to never let them spoil
I close the box and I bury it right beneath the soil
They make me strong, they make me brave
They will stay there for long to save
The other night I close my eyes trying hard to sleep
My eyes stay open wide enough, I started counting sheep
The light inside I have, I carry with all this fear
It's shutting down and getting dark, dreams are nowhere near
It was a mistake hiding courage in a cartoon box of dreams
If I'd gather my soul and open that box it would be easier than it seems
The voice in my head is forcing me saying, 'No!'
I don't really care at all and all I do is go
I search the grounds at every place
I hope my dreams were not replaced
I saw a light under the ground
My box of dreams is what I found.

Katie Chrobok (12)
International School of Prague, Prague

Hope And Reality

Bustling noises of footsteps make clouds of dust on the floor.
A few loud dry laughters and lectures near the door.
Time passes by, with every second, hour, day being the same,
Forgetting their exceptional dream that was full with the desires of flames.

Taunting whispers of desire and dream linger closely
Tapping against firmly closed door of my heart
Tender spirits are blown away harshly
Torn along by the blades of reality and duty.

Can we ever get back to the youngest, brightest age of our life?
Can we heal the scratches of pain that we must endure?
Careless teardrops of agony fall down
Carefully signalling to continue the broken life of our young trees to grow.

Seoyoung Lee (13)
International School of Prague, Prague

The Key

What if the world was a square
And an apple tasted like a pear?
What if you went to school at night
And seeing sunlight would give you a fright?
What if having a friend was an insult
And what if you were born as an adult?
What if your whole life is a dream
And no one is on the same team?
What if you're happy when you are alone
And everyone speaks in monotone?
And what if I wasn't with you
Then my whole life I would be blue,
Anything I would do for you,
But for you I couldn't even name three,
But to open my heart once again I would need you,
The key.

Ben Sapir (12)
International School of Prague, Prague

The Moon And Back

You hold the key to my heart
I don't think we could ever be apart
I love you to the moon and back
And our friendship could never crack

Our friendship means so much to me
I don't think you would disagree
It cannot be bought or sold
We'll be best friends until we're old.

Forever is how long we'll be together
I love you, my treasure
Not sisters by blood
But always sisters by heart.

Anna Sheridan (12)
International School of Prague, Prague

Mistakes Made 100 Years Ago

Life
It is the thing that always gets in the way
Of getting to live forever
Life is living until you die
Everyone wants to live forever
To fix the mistakes
They made a hundred years ago
But once a mistake is made
The damage is done
You can never fix a mistake
You can only patch it up
You can only cover up the hole you made in your history
Mistakes
It is the thing that always gets in the way
Of keeping the world
A better world.

Suri Celia Ridder (12)
International School of Prague, Prague

Dauntless, Erudite Or Amity

My future is so unclear,
My eyes are flooding with tears,
My legs are shaking,
I can't walk, I'm struggling.

All my dreams have shattered,
My hopes have scattered,
Everyone's asking,
Inside I'm panicking.

They say it's not a big deal,
But I still haven't healed,
I wonder what faction is meant for me,
Dauntless, Erudite or Amity?

Gaurangi Kaushik (12)
International School of Prague, Prague

What Is Life?

Imagine life as a stage,
Where unpredictable things can happen,
Imagine life as an ocean,
Filled with islands,
Where is your island?
Life is like a story,
To be told to your children,
Life is like a watermelon,
Getting eaten with bitter and sweet parts.
Life could be like that,
Life . . . is very imaginable too.
Our lives are special,
No two are the same.
How do you imagine life?
Now imagine . . .

Hali Chen (11)
International School of Prague, Prague

Silence

Silence.
Overpowering.
Feelings and emotions.
My mind is blank.
Darkness is overpowering.
My head is about to explode,
Thoughts rush in.
Thoughts rush out.
Darkness looms over me.
I am helpless.
I am an ant, nowhere to hide.
All is crushed, I am crushed.
I can't believe silence is so loud.

Zahra Rawji (12)
International School of Prague, Prague

Bankruptcy

An empire that once ruled the world,
Spawning inventors, philosophers and gold,
In '81 it joined the EU,
Borrowed, invested and grew.

Greece is a marvellous place
Due to go bankrupt in June.
Germany is hot on the chase
And help can't come too soon.
The Greeks now show their other face
With Syria trying to change the tune.

The people want dignity,
To create their own destiny.
With 400 billion outstanding loan
No wonder the Greeks do nothing but moan.

James E P Neale (12)
International School of Prague, Prague

Imaginary Place

Cold air brushes against my face
Thoughts cloud my mind
I do not feel in place
Instead rather confined
My hands become cold
And as I get near
I tighten my hold
People start to appear
I slow my pace
I want it to last
This imaginary place
Although it has passed
Its remains still stay
And will never die away.

Mila Virk (12)
International School of Prague, Prague

NYC

My city, New York, is full of dreams
and all the skyscrapers have glowing beams.
New York is full of smiles,
that go on for miles.
This city has outstanding fashion,
as well as that it has lots of action.
It is full of success,
if you are new to it you will be in stress.
New York is a city that you will want to be in
and it is only getting better, not like it has been.
New York is a city full of hope,
is there any better place? Nope!

Zachary Yemets (11)
International School of Prague, Prague

Snow

When the snow falls to the ground,
When the world is white,
With children all around,
The snow glistening in the sunlight.

Though the crisp, cold air is like a wasp waiting to sting,
The snow is a gift from the wide, open sky,
With each snowflake a glistening jewel,
Be ever so grateful for the joy it will bring,
For the snow could go, without saying goodbye,
So be grateful for snow, don't be a fool.

Olivia Nicole Ercolino (12)
International School of Prague, Prague

Basketball

Basketball, it's an incredible sport.
Using speed and control up and down the court.
The ball is passed to me and as usual I think if I should shoot.
As I dribble the ball around my pick I think, *should I bail?*
As the ball is released from the grip of my hand I think, *wow was that a fail?*
The ball swishes in the basket with relief rushing through me.
Why isn't everyone looking at me like I am best?
I realised then that it was just a test.
I see my coach screaming at me
And I realised I scored on my own hoop.

Joseph Demirel (13)
International School of Prague, Prague

Ode To The Xbox

Dear Xbox,
My precious, every day we meet.
Seconds, sometimes minutes, hours it may be.
I will keep enjoying the endless worlds we see.
Dying we do together.
Merciless I throw you a little faster than a feather
But in love pain has no place to be
And I know you will be the one that will always rely on me.
My parents might not love you, but I do with all my heart.
Xbox, dear Xbox, I hope we will never be apart.

Max De Jong (12)
International School of Prague, Prague

The Graveyard

Life is a game
A beautiful lie
Full of shame
And still so lame
Afraid of death
That lies ahead
In the darkness
You feel the pain
Of all the loved ones
That passed away.

Kasper Nilsson (11)
International School of Prague, Prague

Winter

I am locked inside a deep cage,
a cage to never be opened.
The key to opening the cage,
has never been spoken.
The frost, the white,
the sharp cold wind.
I will wait,
until it dies.
Spring please come,
winter please end.

Alana Monks (12)
International School of Prague, Prague

Divergent

The sky is getting dark,
The wind is getting stronger.

I can't stay positive any longer
My mind is full with thoughts that
I don't know what to do with
Sometimes happy, sometimes sad and emotionless.

I consider if I should do it or not
I make myself trust that it is just a game
This is called divergent.

Hayeong Ryu (13)
International School of Prague, Prague

You Are Yourself

You are a sentence,
You are a character,
You are a stage,
You are a mirror.
But when you
Feel blue, remember,
You are really
Just you.

Rozalie Benova (12)
International School of Prague, Prague

Dog Days

When I was younger,
I was forever told to get a lock,
Because the monster under my bed
Was only for my midnight eyes.

When I was younger,
I had gone through many toothbrushes.
People always said that forcing your problems out
Was better than giving out broken pieces.

When I was younger,
I was told to save my money.
They taught you the only tortures you had to suffer
Were the ones where you paid the madman.

When I was younger,
I had always dreamed of growing up.
Yet even with one foot in the grave,
They still treated me like the child I internally was.

Rebecca Jenkins (12)
Kemnay Academy, Inverurie

Summer

You make my life extraordinary
Relaxing noises from beaches
And laughter from children.

You bring laughter to every family in the world,
It's as warm as the sun.

A time to laugh and spend with friends,
To eat whatever you want but . . .

When September comes school comes back!
And summer dies.

Pilar López Marchena (12)
King's College Alicante, Alicante

Not Fair

He was in the street painting the walls
While I was cleaning toilets,
Not fair. Not fair.
I take the gun, as dangerous as a snake,
He had a little knife like a three-year-old boy,
I had to do something to teach him,
I had to do something.

He was with a girl,
While I was with a sick boy,
Not fair. Not fair.
I take the mobile phone as dangerous as a snake,
He had a beer in his hand like a teenager.
I had to do something to teach him,
I had to do something.

He was drunk in the disco,
While I was laying a blanket over a sick boy,
Not fair. Not fair.
I take a lighter as dangerous as a snake,
He had a motorbike with a girl like a boy in his twenties.
I had to do something to teach him,
I had to do something.

He was sleeping,
While I was preparing breakfast,
Not fair. Not fair.
I take the car, as dangerous as a snake,
He takes a gun like a man and gets in a fight.
I had to do something to teach him,
I had to do something.

He was dying with a bullet in his heart,
While I was sleeping,
Not fair. Not fair.
I researched the Internet as thorough as I can,
He takes a breath like a dying man.
I had to do something to teach him,
I had to do something.

Pedro Alemañ Serna (12)
King's College Alicante, Alicante

The Broken Princess

Have you ever had to put up with bullying?
Never fitting in?
No?
Well I have
And it hurts.

Teenage hood is like a sparkling flame lighting up in the dark,
When everything changes and goes by,
An era of desperation.

I'm afraid he won't notice me,
I'm afraid I'll break,
Putting up with this,
All day.

Then it gets worse,
Having to get up every morning knowing this will happen,
There are cruel people in this world,
Never forget it.

Princes, princesses, villains and sidekicks,
We all have a fairy tale to be told.

In my fairy tale . . .

The typical cool boy that thinks of himself as the best,
Is the villain.

The people who laugh at his jokes,
Afraid of not fitting in, are the sidekicks.

These are a special category,
They hurt because of their own weak self-confidence,
They hurt others to make them feel small.

My prince will be charming and intelligent,
He will care and defend people who are being used,
Maybe I've met him before or maybe not,
Who knows?

I'm the princess,
Misunderstood, broken,
I'm a broken princess,
I'm a broken princess, in my broken world,
In my broken palace and broken room,

Brokenly curled.

Have you ever wondered what other people feel?
Have you ever wondered what's it like to be me?
Having to fight this all day long?
Well it hurts.

Try to be the broken princess in the broken world,
Afraid they'll discover what I truly am,
Battling myself,
Controlling,
I'm afraid that if I show my true colours,
People will laugh,
But what can I say,
I'm a teenager,
Isn't it supposed to be this way?

Aitana Cirauqui Palmero (12)
King's College Alicante, Alicante

Politics In Spain

Oh dear Spain
You've been great
We could've been rich
We could've been powerful
But now we're a poodle
Some of us are undesirable
Some of us are honest
But not many
We are in crisis
Zapatero's fault
And now we have Rajoy
Another one of the same pile
The new one is Podemos
The new political party
They're popular
They filled 'La Puerta del Sol' in Madrid
With followers.

Alejandro Bürg López (12)
King's College Alicante, Alicante

Mr Hodges

Oh Mr Hodges,
I still hate your stupid and pathetic shiny bald head,
Even though I got in trouble,
For saying what I thought about it.
Never mind.

Oh Mr Hodges,
You are as dirty as a big pig,
You never hear, or answer me back,
It seems as if you had a problem in your ear,
Just because at class,
You don't hear my fear.
Possibly.

I still remember that hilarious moment,
When you made me pay for my maths book,
It committed suicide,
My maths book had many algebra problems,
But, you did not believe me.
Normal.

Oh Mr Hodges,
You are as intelligent as a grumpy donkey,
You think you have much maths knowledge,
But really, you should go back to college.
Sure.

I will not let your stupid exams enter my brain,
I've just burned them with blue flame.

Oh Mr Hodges,
You are as strict as a general,
Every minute you set homework, again and again,
Each time more and more,
So don't ask yourself why so many people faint on the floor.

The worst thing in your class is studying,
People say, it is worse than bullying.
Believe me.

I am told from you I am a lie,
I am told from you I am no one,
I am told from you that I will never leave college alive.

Oh Mr Hodges,
You are a ghost,
You bring bad luck,
Do you remember you had a gypsy curse,
You frightened everyone and stole their purse.

Oh Mr Hodges,
You have been fired!
Let's celebrate your absence!

Óscar Bou Belda (12)
King's College Alicante, Alicante

Why Would I Love You?

You're so sweet
I can't resist
I write you this
Because I love you.

You're so sweet
Like chocolate
Your blond hair
As shiny as the sunrise.

You're so sweet
Like a strawberry
I will love you
Till the world ends.

You're so sweet
Like golden syrup
You're mine,
Only mine.

You're so sweet
I can't resist
Your messages
Are so romantic.

Why would I love you?

Mireia Suarez (12)
King's College Alicante, Alicante

Oh, Brother

Oh brother
Oh brother
No one asked me
For your presence

But now you're gone to university
Everyone celebrates
Your distance

And don't expect
Mum and Dad
To call you
Because they have
Blocked you

Or was it me
That blocked the lines?
Because if I did
I did it fast

Like a leopard on the run,
I caught you
Crunch, munch
Yum, yum, yum

Talking about the Devil!
You big pig
You ate my last doughnut

But who cares?
You've gone
I get to keep your room
With double the fun

OK this poem is a bit mean
But understand
We are mortal enemies

I've got to admit I'm a bit sad
But let's celebrate
You're gone, bam!

Alejandro Perea Millson (12)
King's College Alicante, Alicante

A Lake Of Red

Dash of chainmail,
Tinkle, tinkle,
Swords shining in the bright,
The constant march of soldiers,
And orders bellowed by the leader,
One, two, one, two,
Booming, dashing, crashing,
Howling of the horns,
The moaning of horses,
Neigh,
Stop.

Anticipation,
Worried looks from one to other,
Clouds grabbing at the sun,
It's not long now,
Before the
Shouting, screaming,
Bits of wood,
From punished shields,
Spears and corpses far beneath,
And lakes,
Of crimson red.

Death surrounds the field,
Clouds push away,
Peace but at a price too high,
And as the sun sets,
Red the sunset is,
From so much blood spilled,
By brave, honest men,
Sent to die by wealthy fools,
Sat on a throne,
Whose worries are only money,
Cashing!

Mark Leonov (12)
King's College Alicante, Alicante

Hugging My Legs

Me,
Sitting lonely,
No one likes me,
Everyone thinks I'm an alien,
They look at me,
They look at me with those glaring eyes,
They're conscious of it,
So conscious that they emphasise it,
Again and again.

They think I'm going to cry,
They're so right,
But I put my mask on,
That special mask that only bullied and hated people have.
What they see is just a face,
Inside . . . oh inside,
They don't have a clue of what's going on,
If they could imagine,
If only.
My world,
It's falling apart,
Bit by bit,
It's like taking off a plaster,
The slower, the more it hurts.

And there they are,
Shining at the top of popularity,
They can manipulate everybody.
Pupils, of their class, lower year groups, higher ones.
Basically everyone,
And here's me,
Hugging my legs.

Lorena Galvañ Miguel (12)
King's College Alicante, Alicante

Why Bother?

Mum I'm fed up of you,
Why bother?
Your hatred was as terrifying as fire
As scary as ghosts,
Why bother?
I hate you!
When I was alone
You were never there
To help me,
Why bother?

Your heart was as strong as rock
As hard as steel,
You never showed emotion
I'm tired of you Mum!
Why bother?

But now that I'm alone
I feel empty,
Without forgetting my hate
As if you were a pathetic, crooked dragon,
Why bother?

I'm tired of you,
You were never there
And you never will be
You were an annoyance,
Why bother?
Really Mum, listen! Why bother?

Carlos Meana Pastor (12)
King's College Alicante, Alicante

Shadows

I'm seldom seen at all,
Just like a shadow on the wall,
You don't see me standing there,
Or you do but just don't care.
I'm walking through the corridor
Just like all of you,
You don't seem to notice me,
Why, aren't I a human too?
I just want to be accepted,
In this world we call school
But you point and laugh at me,
And I feel like a fool.
So I keep to the darkness,
Never to be seen,
So I keep in the darkness,
Never in-between,
Where the people are laughing,
I hide away
From the people who are smiling
And now even today,
I'm beginning to accept
This is how it will be,
My life forever
So yay, lucky me . . .

Kyla Watkins (12)
King's College Alicante, Alicante

Why Can't I Have You?

Oh sweetheart,
You're an angel falling from the sky,
As sweet as the sweetest pie.

My little princess,
You're as sweet as caramel,
I love you,
I will love you till I die.

I need you here
To not freeze
Like a cold ice slice.

Oh my celestial god,
You're so sweet,
I can't resist,
I want you here,
I need you here,
My beautiful baby.

I know I can't have you
But I'm frozen without you,
Come home with me,
And let's be together forever.
Who cares?
I can't have you.

Virginia Domingo García (13)
King's College Alicante, Alicante

Treasures

You hear a whisper,
You hear a tinkle,
You hear it tripping, dripping,
A sprinkle.

It's unique,
It's fabulous,
It's nevertheless,
It's never the more.
It's overrated,
For evermore.

What else can I say about it?
It's mine, only mine.
It's a treasure that I keep,
Which continues to shine.

I keep it to myself,
So that no one can see,
The treasures it holds,
Which are only for me.

You're wondering what it is,
But I'm not going to tell you.
I'm leaving you in awe,
To make you wonder.

Carla Navarro (12)
King's College Alicante, Alicante

No One Will See Me

I sit all alone,
Another day,
Hugging myself,
Crying a river.

People don't see me,
They probably think
I'm not even there.

People don't care,
They talk about things,
No one cares,
Then someone spots me.

They kick me,
They hurt me,
They crack up,
My heart.

A river I cry,
All alone,
Hugging my heart
Hoping that
No one will see me,
No one.

Luna Quesada (12)
King's College Alicante, Alicante

The Horrible Day

Oh no, not again.
The bully has arrived.
I hate him,
He's the last person I would want to be,
In my whole, whole life!

I usually wonder if he's a boy or a devil.
He smells of rotten fish.
When I start to smell that horrible odour,
The siren inside my head turns on.

This is when I take off the brake and accelerate.
I start sprinting like Usain Bolt.
It usually takes me thirty-three seconds
To get the books out of the locker
And run away to class.

Unfortunately, this wouldn't last forever.
The day arrived.
It was a rainy day.
I was at the lockers and I slipped.
The bully arrived, he started lifting me
Until I was nearly bleeding.
And then the teachers laughed at me.

Pablo Pereda Asencio (12)
King's College Alicante, Alicante

Oh School

Why weekend, why?
Why are you so short?
Why do we only have two days at weekends
And five of week days?

Oh weekend,
You enter my heart
On Friday afternoon,
Oh weekend you make me happy.

Why school, why?
Why are you so long?
Why do we have tests
And homework?

Oh school,
You enter to the heart of evil
On Monday morning,
Oh school, you make me sad.

Alejandro Lopez Ortega (12)
King's College Alicante, Alicante

Josh's Journey

Josh was alone
In a corner crying.
He was bullied.
He doesn't go to class sometimes.
Angry as a lion in a fight.

Josh cries a lot
As loudly as a peal of bells
Always eating at a table alone
Never eating a lot.

Josh plays alone
He doesn't play sport
He plays with his own figures
In a corner.

When he goes home
He walks a long way
He is always bullied
In the end.

Victor Martinez Perez (12)
King's College Alicante, Alicante

The Truth About Peaches

Oh peach,
I love the way you are made,
your flavour is as tasty as the best chocolate
I wouldn't change you for anything.
You are as precious to me as gold.

I love your little hairs
so sweet, so sweet.
I became as still as a mannequin
the first time I saw you.

You make me happy each time I'm sad.
Oh peach, you illuminate my brain and make me think.

My eyes freeze like a slice of ice
each time I look at you.
Your bright orange colour
illuminates the dark.

You are just perfect.

Rodrigo Campos (13)
King's College Alicante, Alicante

Christmas, I Love Christmas

You love Christmas
I love Christmas
I am happy
You are happy
It's a celebration to be together
Children singing
Birds flapping
Everyone is here
Because they are happy.

Everyone is dancing in the mirror
Singing in the shower
It's Christmas, Christmas
As sweet as a sweet
As cold as me
I am with Santa
As red as a heart
I am with Santa but I prefer presents.

Carla Palmi Alonso (12)
King's College Alicante, Alicante

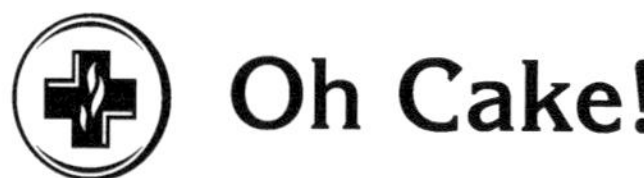

Oh Cake!

Oh cake,
You are the one who makes children laugh
You are the one that always sees children smile
When they see you they are overcome with joy.

Oh cake,
You are the sweetest
You are as sweet as sugar from the sky
When you are made from chocolate . . .
Children's hearts thump madly.

Oh cake,
Sweet moments happen when you are there
Your spongy and creamy layers are outstanding
You captivate us
And bring us back to life.

I hope one day you are mine
Oh cake.

Libertad Sempere Baña (12)
King's College Alicante, Alicante

Inside The Father's Heart

What about you and I?
Why you just wanna lie?
Don't you know that I know
All about that dirty cry?

I loved, I felt, but now I'm in fear.
You wanted to be with him, dear?
But now there is no way back.
So just stay there and think about that.

I still remember the crystal eyes,
And a bomb inside my heart.
But now, the bomb has exploded,
There is no return, no happy way back.

Why do I still suffer?
You don't remember me
But something in my heart tells me
That you need me.
Even though I'm the grave,
Looking for my daughter's happiness.

Stefania Buzykanova (12)
King's College Alicante, Alicante

Oh Chocolate!

I look at you wrapped in seducing paper
Staring at me from the candy machine.

I can buy a chocolate for my sister later
Who lives with a big family in Bream.

Today I hunger for you to lift me up
And make me fly from this scene.

Why do I have to be good
When nobody else is clean?

Marie-Theres Rundkvist (13)
King's College Alicante, Alicante

The Waste Of War

It starts with a little argument,
And ends with the spread of death and horror . . .
You don't know how it feels,
When blood gets spilled.

Bang!
Bang!
Boom!
Then all you notice is silence,
People crying, people flying to Heaven.
Those poor people as innocent as birds.

They suffer and stagger to survive,
Bullets sprinting towards their heads.
Fire crackling, burning, killing, threatening.
How do you feel about it?
How do you feel about them?
The anger of war!

Adrien Venot Marco (12)
King's College Alicante, Alicante

War

War is death
Death means suffering
Arms kill people
People are you

People are dying
And you are in your house
Watching television
But you could be next,
You could die!

While you are reading this poem,
Children are dying.

Álvaro Barroso Lopez (12)
King's College Alicante, Alicante

Our World

We don't need violence,
We don't need misery,
We don't need poverty,
No avarice.

When everything has been in vain,
When everything has become hatred,
They struggle to survive the pain,
Poverty, chaos, sorrow, hopes delayed.

Who is guilty?
Who will take the blame,
Everybody's lives are the same,
Why not stop this?

Because then we all walk hand in hand with faith
Searching for the same eternal peaceful place.

Manuela Trindade Lobraico (12)
King's College Alicante, Alicante

The Fight

We win,
We fight,
With all our might
And what is this terrible sin?

We lose,
We hurt,
We've gone berserk,
And our memory's bruised.

Not one grin,
Not one night,
We go without the fight,
This line is drawing thin.

Chloe Murray (12)
King's College Alicante, Alicante

Oh Elena

Oh Elena,
You're so sweet like chocolate
When I taste it
It reminds me of the taste of your rose-red lips.
Your eyes are brown like a sleek cat.
Your skin is cream coloured
Like the delicious milk I drink.
Oh Elena,
You're so beautiful like the moon
When I gaze upon it
You remind me of cake
Your hair is black like the night
Your voice is amazing that you win my kiss.
Oh Elena.

Ian Harris Benitez (12)
King's College Alicante, Alicante

You

I looked into your eyes,
But I got lost,
I came closer to your lips
So I could observe the love you breathe out as you looked at me
Each of our heartbeats were heard in the world's silence,
Or simply we were in our own world
Until the moment your lips touched mine
I suddenly changed the world.
But I was just trying to concentrate on your lips
That were now going backwards.
Your lips' taste faded
And you ran away into the darkness
And stayed there forever.
But someday I think the darkness will come back.

Alba De Haan Sánchez (12)
King's College Alicante, Alicante

Time Concealed Our Fate

That last summer
Your steps were as quick and light as the clouds in the sky.
The blocky, childish letters you wrote,
Were like beacons of hope in my eyes.
You taught me how to live in the moment since it all would be over too soon
Your smile remains in my heart.

The days I spent with you burned their imprint onto my heart.
I will always feel them though my memories may fade
I just don't know how to express my love for you
I never could but I hope you'd understand
This aching pain in my chest.

Each night took us further away from each other.
Those transcended words you spoke so carefreely through your opaque heart.
Even now I embrace your words in my heart
Upholding our future, you and I fell in love
Your trembling voice, your faded eyes
Even now I try to look for them . . .

Uncertainly I ran after you in that crowd of strangers,
Desperately seeking
These unknown feelings I have locked inside of me

That magical unknown place we found on that day
Knowing our feelings, we ignored all
Even now that light continues to shine
Through that same path.

You taught me how to express this love I had for you
Pushing me forward, always being there,
I keep asking the same question,
Where are you?
Are you somewhere in this endless sky?

Knowing the answer burns my heart
The days I spent with you burned their imprint onto my heart,
I will always feel them though my memories may fade.
Even if I jump into the future,
You will always be special and precious to me
I cannot erase you from my mind,
Even though I try so hard

The sky goes on,
Endlessly time passes,
Each day
That I met in the vastness of time,
Was the greatest experience of my life

I will embrace this life without you,
Living each moment endlessly
This endless sky holds precious memories,
As I hold these precious memories close,
To my heart
I will never forget that summer's day,
When you confessed your love for me.

As the seasons change, as time flows on,
Tears spill from my eyes
I will always look for the forgotten memories of my soul
Remembering your smile that day,
I treasure it in my beating heart.

Disguising myself was the only thing I was good at
Though I may fall in love again,
You will eternally hold a place
In the deepest part of my soul
I will keep searching for those unspoken words you said that day
Time concealed our fate
I just want to meet you now . . .

Arfa Siddique (13)
King's Park Secondary School, Glasgow

Tomorrow's Another Day

As I look into her eyes all that I can see,
Is a little child who just needs someone to do her a good deed.
Her dad is not around anymore,
Her mother doesn't care.
She blames her for the fact her dad left last year.
She takes care of her siblings, makes them promise not to tell,
She knows Mum will get angry and make their life hell.

When she goes to school the children laugh
She sits by herself at the back of the class,
Desperately waiting for 4 o'clock to come
She hides in an alley waiting for lunch to pass,
And hides in shadows when people walk past.

Don't let them see you're hurting, don't tell them about your pain,
They will only ask questions and Mum brings out the cane
Just pick your head up and smile,
Don't care about what they say,
Just keep on remembering tomorrow's another day.

Stephanie Eregbu (13)
King's Park Secondary School, Glasgow

My Brother

My brother
Makes me angry
Until I break
He annoys me
He makes me break things
I shout at him
He angers me so much
I could go red
And blow up
Like a volcano.

Will Vickrage (12)
Mearns Academy, Laurencekirk

Swimming

Swimming
It's my favourite sport.
I go three times
A week.
Train at Montrose Leisure Centre.
My coach
Incredibly strict.
No one worse than her!
I love swimming
Well it's a sport
You need.
It's as important
As our eyesight.
Got offered to be
In the team.
Shocked.

Shannon Tait (12)
Mearns Academy, Laurencekirk

What About Now?

Empty stars in our hands,
Ways I loved it.
All the things that we are
But are not saying.
Ways it made me feel alive
Let's do it one more time,
All the things it could be.
If it fell one more time
It was going to this point,
I will find it, now that's here,
There is nothing to fear,
It will free us.

Jack Robb (12)
Mearns Academy, Laurencekirk

History Was Made

130 years of pain and disappointment
Only silverware can ease the pain
On the 17th May in a rainy Glasgow
How that pain went away
The super Saints went all the way
On Scottish Cup Final day
Determination won the game
Andos' header and McLean's ricochet
There was no way back for the Arabs on the day
The cup was won, the Saints were dynamite
St Johnstone's name was engraved
On the trophy for evermore
History was made on that day.

James-Joseph Stewart (13)
Mearns Academy, Laurencekirk

Forest

Trees stood still
Like nut shells
Birds flutter
Between trees
Flowers like
Colourful snowy lakes
Waterfall drips
Onto smooth marble
Wood that smells
Like peaches.

Reece Ian McDonald (12)
Mearns Academy, Laurencekirk

Awake

Owls awake
In the night
Hooting
Noisy but soothing
Eyes are watching
Bright orange eyes
Peek out of the trees
In the warm summer nights
Owls awake.

April Lindsay (12)
Mearns Academy, Laurencekirk

Teenagers

I like being a teenager
Young and free
I hate being a teenager
Everything is disappearing
Does not come back
Meeting new friends is fun
Trying new things
Some you hate
Some you love.

Samantha Whyte (12)
Mearns Academy, Laurencekirk

The Perfect Couple

They are the perfect couple
Like mash and gravy
Put together so greatly
Just meant to be.
Love in life and death
So young
Don't be dumb.
So you can marry
And be so happy.

Brendan Deeney (12)
Mearns Academy, Laurencekirk

Swimming

Swimming
My favourite hobby
I like backstroke
Front crawl and
Doggy paddling
I like the water on my toes
Feels funny
Like swimming with my friends, fun
We get to muck about.

Devon Jackson (12)
Mearns Academy, Laurencekirk

The Anger

Waiting to lash out like a bomb ticking away
School makes me angry
Can't concentrate
Can't get work done
It really annoys me
I throw things, I scream and shout
I get frustrated
I hate school so much.

Tracy Reid (12)
Mearns Academy, Laurencekirk

Glory

Scottish Cup shines
And gleams like the sun.
Two teams play against each other
Fans support their team.
Cheering when they score.
Getting angry with the referee
Giving the other team a free kick.

Lee McWilliam (12)
Mearns Academy, Laurencekirk

Ebola Poem

Ebola
Worst disease
Based in West Africa
Kills and spreads
But can we find a cure?

Kai Henderson (12)
Mearns Academy, Laurencekirk

Prisoner

Video after video they spread the word,
In a trolley their heads get transferred,
Here life is terribly bad,
Nothing like the life we used to have,
Every day I pray to gods to let me go home,
But I'm stuck here in the middle of a war zone,
My family, my family, I hope they're okay,
Now I don't care if my son is gay,
Out here for work,
That's all it was,
Now I don't even have food to put in my jaws.

Punch after punch,
Whip after whip,
Someone tell these monsters to just get a grip!
My body is now slashed, scarred, cut and red,
Right now I wish I was really just dead.
That beast of a man,
The leader they call he,
Points to my best friend, whose name is Archie,
They beat him down, put a bag over his head,
It looks like Archie's gonna be the next one dead.

He had left my view, I heard his screams,
Or was it the young girls that came here to fulfil their dreams?
The place went quiet.

From behind me I heard the assistant say,
'That one there, the fat man.'
I turned to see a swinging baseball bat!

I woke to see the beheader staring right at me,
He kicked me in the back then I fell to my knees,
Oh no, oh dear, the camera and the red light was on,
It was finally my turn from this world to be gone . . .

A prisoner.

Brodie Mackay (13)
Musselburgh Grammar School, Musselburgh

The Man

The man burst in, wielding a gun at the frightened family
Only his eyes were showing, wide and mad,
The rest of his face was covered in a black cloth.
The woman stands protectively in front of her two children
Who are huddled behind her in the corner . . .
She won't be for long though . . .
Blood flows from the two holes in her chest,
The man laughs. The children scream.
The woman falls to the ground . . .

The older child runs forward and drops to the floor beside his dead mother,
He screams at her, begging her to stand up,
To speak, to breathe again . . . nothing . . .
He rises, rage all over his young face,
Like a horse out of the gate he starts for the man,
Leaving his young sister still petrified and screaming in the corner,
He gets no more than three paces before he has two bullets
Imbedded in his brain and falls to the ground beside his mother . . .

The man cackles again and starts towards the small girl,
He picks her up by her throat and dangles her tiny body
Three feet above the ground, at eye level,
Dropping his gun to his side, he shakes the young girl,
Her screams fill the otherwise empty, silent night,
Nobody comes to the rescue of the innocent family,
The girl falls silent and goes limp,
The man throws her down on the ground,
He picks up his weapon and turns towards the door,
He stops momentarily to take in the sight of what he has done,
The boy and woman lying in an ever increasing pool of spreading blood,
The looks of fear and anger still anxiously present on their faces,
The girl lies next to them,
Her face still bright scarlet and tear-stained,
Once again the man laughs appreciatively
At his good work and leaves . . .

Lucy Carbray-Johnson (13)
Musselburgh Grammar School, Musselburgh

Housed Bird Monologue – Driven To The Brink

12 long hours . . . stuck in a small cage,
Only a small grey feather ball for company,
What? Now I hear footsteps, coming down the hall,
12 long hours . . . stuck in a small cage,
Excitement floods now, jump, flap, tweet,
My heart beating fast, hearing the drawing feet,
12 long hours . . . stuck in a small cage,
Whoosh! Off come the rug,
Clang! of clunks, the two heavy catches,
Swoop! Down comes the big human hands,
Hiss! I try and ward it off – but fast on it comes,
Waaa! It caught me! I hiss, I struggle, I bite,
12 long hours . . . stuck in a small cage,
Now I'm stuck in some human's sweaty hands,
Yes! He let me go, but now I only have a room to fly,
Only a small room to fly, only a small room to swoop,
Not such a space to do a loop-de-loop,
Now I have that feather ball flapping in my face,
Trying to make the humans love him, love him in my place!
But as everybody knows, no bird slips under my toes,
The humans are gone, my plan in action, time to start,
I lure him to the kitchen, through the open door,
Show him the fish, make him want a dish, as he peers,
Push him forward, jump on the lid, now the fish won't be the only dish . . .

Daniel Simpson (13)
Musselburgh Grammar School, Musselburgh

Paris – 10th January

Paris, it's normally the city of love
But not today,
Today, twelve have been brutally murdered
Why though?
How have they ended up in the red,
How have they ended up dead?

All they were doing was their job,
Drawing cartoons for the people
But they can't draw Mohammed,
They supposedly were racist,
But to who?
Not the Muslims anyway,
As the Quran does not say,
That he cannot be drawn.

These imbeciles who call themselves Muslim,
Are no more Muslim than I,
As the Quran states not to kill the innocent,
Not even to kill,
For what did the workers of Charlie Hebdo do,
What did they do to deserve this?
Why? Why?

Connor Cranston (13)
Musselburgh Grammar School, Musselburgh

Pizza

I love his cheesy jokes,
I love his rosy, red cheeks.
I love his squishy face,
I love his pineapple hair.
I love his sparkling teeth like mushy mushrooms
But most of all I love that he is a pizza!

Abbie Burstow (13)
Musselburgh Grammar School, Musselburgh

New York Snow

Once in New York there was snow
Which caused lots of problems you know
Like slipping and tripping
And lorries were flipping
Such a treacherous place to go

The snow wouldn't stop falling down
There were no smiles to see just frowns
Their fingers were numb
Wind hit like a drum
No people or kids were around

The schools, they closed for the day
The children, they shouted hooray
Although they were cold
They were brave and bold
Threw snowballs as part of their play

After days the missed sun came up
Hot chocolate stopped filling the cups
The children came out
People happy no doubt
Because they could start earning bucks.

Matthew Scott (13)
Musselburgh Grammar School, Musselburgh

Blue Oceans Of Sky

The spluttery start is the beginning of a journey into other lands;
a way of travelling into kingdoms unknown
and the way of showing travellers a different life.
The metallic cone-shaped flyer is the means of getting there,
lumbering in a rattly ascent into the blue oceans of sky.
Once airborne a sense of relief escapes the mouths of flyers
but all eyes are transfixed on their home nation,
slowly disappearing into a continuous smudge.
Life, heat and memories all are stopped in time
as this unnatural flyer pierces its way through the Atlantic of skies.
The horizon is its only way of distinguishing sea and air.
This sensation goes on for some time yet.
The rocky silhouette is the only clear sign of land
and produces a sense of longing with it.
Flyers end their mid-life on the plane and brace for the impact of landing,
still not on new ground, but almost.
Tension builds as it comes closer and closer,
hands digging into fabric as ears pop.
Bump is the sign and a second sigh of relief is released
at the first close-up look at a new nation's beauty.

Keir Hendrie (13)
Musselburgh Grammar School, Musselburgh

Ode To A Fairytale

Once upon a time
Rainbows would shine,
And unicorns pranced about
Princesses would gaze,
Out at the sunset haze
As their princes slayed dragons
Oh, they had a fantastic time
But that was all, once upon a time.

Now fairy tales are different
Most females take the lead
Freeing all the districts
Now they no longer need
Princes, castles or saviours
They can do it all alone
While we sit reading, watching
Their stories from our homes.
It could be us someday,
Our stories told far and wide,
Stories about these heroes
And the secrets they may hide.

Morven Thomson (13)
Musselburgh Grammar School, Musselburgh

New Season

After the death of her brother she still comes bright
Replacing black with yellow and darkness with light
She brings the animals with her and the sun
She even grows the flowers and the trees
Still she misses her brother dearly
She mourns him, wearing black
But after a while still comes back bright
So RIP to winter but spring brings life.

Mairi Goodall (13)
Musselburgh Grammar School, Musselburgh

Demons Inside

Demons.
Demons inside my head.
Judging me and everything I do.
I know they're not real but they still torment me.

I'm not like most other people.
I see things differently.
You see a knife.
I see relief,
Relief from this pain and suffering.

One cut, two cuts, three.
Blood and tears drip to the floor.
Drip after drip after drip.
I watch the red trickle from my wrist
And pain fades away
Like the sun fades into the darkness.

Demons.
Demons inside my head.
I try my best,
But there's no escape.

Evie Thomson (13)
Musselburgh Grammar School, Musselburgh

Fearful France

Shots fired as loud as thunder
The people here come to murder
Red blood lay on the ground
Hostages taken, bodies found
The police raid
And this story does not fade
The people of France must move on
A day at a time, life goes on.

Jake Allan (13)
Musselburgh Grammar School, Musselburgh

11:02, 9th August 1945

Misty clouds roll in as the day opens
As thousands wake
So too does the city

A mother nurtures her angelic baby
A father sends his daughter to school
Workers drearily trudge to work
Their silent convoys making streaks through the city
Pupils meander grudgingly to school
Their dismal faces reeking with monotony.

The virgin morning is crisp and sweet
The sky is cloudy, yet bright all the same
Its light flooding the land with its pastel hues
The wind is silent like a mouse, yet heard all the same
Its ethereal tendrils, tickling the trees

The morning is normal, quiet and plain
Everyone is busy, unsuspecting of what's to come
Then a deafening roar shatters the sky
And a thousand cries go silent.

Cameron Henderson (13)
Musselburgh Grammar School, Musselburgh

Anime – Death Note

Demons of darkness and death
Everyone running in fear
Are we not all evil?
Tell me who to write
Hatred or for vengeance

No one needs to know
One or a thousand
That won't make a difference
Evil shall prevail!

Sally McKay (13)
Musselburgh Grammar School, Musselburgh

Hate

It's a strange sensation,
You feel it bubbling up inside you,
You turn boiling,
You are dangerously fragile,
One word and you will tip over the edge,
No warning,
No prevention,
Look closely,
You can see it,
Eyes narrowed,
Head beating like a drum,
No matter how much you battle it,
There is no winning,
It is the thing we all hope we aren't,
It is being hated,
Hate is strong and dangerous,
There is no outrunning hate.

Robyn Paterson (13)
Musselburgh Grammar School, Musselburgh

Love

His sharp, white, clean teeth,
Like a flock of sheep.
His blue eyes,
Like the crystal ocean.
His blond hair,
Like a lion's mane.
The way he looks at me,
The way I feel when he does.
Almost like butterflies in my stomach.
This feeling is love!
And I love him!

Ria O'Neill (13)
Musselburgh Grammar School, Musselburgh

My Rabbit

I have a little bunny,
His name is Benji Boo,
He is a black rabbit,
With grey and white bits too.
He likes to run about,
And likes to play in the snow,
But if he tries to get out,
I'm sure he will not go.
He is our family pet,
We love him very much,
But we don't really see him,
As he sits in his hutch.

Siobhan Brett (14)
Musselburgh Grammar School, Musselburgh

Hockey

Hockey, the game of brutal competitors
When attacking your role is to try to score;
You jog first remaining in your giving position
Suddenly you become a bullet shot out of a gun,
Aiming towards the ball, trying to fulfil your ambition
Becoming a harmless thief you rob the ball off the provoked player
Rapidly you are now the hockey ball conveyor
You dribble the ball, dodging people like a criminal dodging the police
Your heart feels at peace
Finally you have the chance to score and you shoot
The ball flies past the goalie and pursues its route to victory.

Niamh Cara Gillan (13)
Musselburgh Grammar School, Musselburgh

Peace

Fight, why do they fight?
Do they not see the outcome of war?
The death, the pain, the bodies all around,
Boots splashing in the blood and tears of friend and foe alike.
Do they not see the monsters they're become?
The suffering they inflict?
Do they not see that they are being played like pawns on a chessboard,
Disposable, expendable?
Fight, why do they fight?

James Hamilton (13)
Musselburgh Grammar School, Musselburgh

Artistic Beauty

They say artists are expressionists
It's more than that The canvas is our life We paint what we see What we feel What we hear We see life in more than just black and white We see the bleakness of the greys And the euphoria of the yellows We live to paint And we paint to live We show you raw emotion through our illustrations We let you judge us, compliment us We stand back while you figure out the meaning Because we know what art is We know what our art is Art is irrational It is passionate It is everything, yet it is nothing Perhaps we paint, sculpt, or draw to find beauty where beauty isn't found Art is what you choose for it to be So decide And then make a difference.

Meghan Timler
North Cape School, Winconsin

Life

Life is something that most people take for granted, Something that can seem too hard for some to carry on forth, Because they are too weak to trudge on, Or they can't bear the pain any more, Something that can be stripped away from people, Sometimes by diseases, Or sometimes by our own race, Sadly but true, Something that fills things, And makes them glow with spirit, While others not,
Something that some risk for others, Something that everything has, Whether they know it or not.

Makenzie Schaal
North Cape School, Wisconsin

Love

He looks at me with his gleaming eyes,
I know his imagination will lead me 'cross the skies. For I like him and want his love, That love you will bring will represent a dove. I look back at him with my bright smile, I know he will be in my heart for a while. Even on a gloomy day, He acts as my light ray. I know he will never make me cry, And it is hurtful to say goodbye. I know he makes my heart glow, But at one point all things you must let go.

Emily Bird
North Cape School, Wisconsin

The Final Seconds

With my bib on I headed onto the court,
My heart was pounding in my chest,
I think I'm going into cardiac arrest,
The crowd was wild,
The air was mild,
I got into position,
I was ready,
The whistle blew.

I was off!
The passing in our team was good,
Taking every chance we could,
The ball came to me,
The chance to shoot was mine,
All of a sudden I launched the ball,
Cheering flooded the whole entire hall,
I had scored!

The ball was back to centre again,
Trying my hardest to fight back the pain,
Darting across the court as fast as lightning,
The other team staring at me, dark and frightening,
I shrugged off the scowls and looks,
My hands wrapped around the ball like fishing hooks,
The umpire was counting, the seconds tick by,
I let go of the ball and watch it fly.

Encouragement from the crowd cheering me on,
The ball slips through the net, the whistle has gone,
The crowd chanting my name,
This truly was an epic game,
Sweat pouring down my face,
Nevertheless we won first place!

Erin McCafferty (12)
Port Glasgow High School, Port Glasgow

Do You Have To?

Do you have to be so mean?
Do you have to be so brutal?
Do you have to show off,
To everyone, everything you see?
Do you have to?

Why is it so entertaining,
Uplifting,
Funny,
To see me upset,
In pain,
As a mess?
Why?

What have I done?
What did I do?
Why is my suffering so satisfying?

Leave me alone?
Leave her and him alone?
Leave us all alone?
Don't get your pleasure from my pain!
Don't get your pleasure from anyone's pain!

Is it because I'm weak?
Is it because I'm not brutal?
Is it because I'm a pushover?
I can be strong,
I can be brutal,
I can stand up for anything I believe in,
Can you?

I may not be the prettiest,
I may not be the smartest,
I may not even be the best arguer,

But at least I accept anyone,
Pretty or not,
Smart or not,
Popular or not,
I accept anyone,
Except you.

Jodie Pollock (12)
Port Glasgow High School, Port Glasgow

Netball

I criss-cross through the players, fighting back the pain
Tears start building up but I just wipe them away
My body is aching and I can't run anymore
But I carry on going, even though I'm sore
My heart is beating faster, *thump, thump, thump*
I know that I can make it, just one more jump!

My legs start moving uncontrollably
All I can think about is the golden trophy
Adrenaline keeps me running through the crowd
I ignore the other team, and their scowls
I throw the ball with all my strength
It flies through the air and lands in the net!

The crowd goes wild and they're jumping up and down
My eyes are shining with happiness and everyone is proud
Everyone is happy, no more pain
I just can't wait to go again!

Abigail Allison (12)
Port Glasgow High School, Port Glasgow

Your Secret Is Safe With Me

Whispers, giggles, she's always by my side.
My emotions from her, I could never hide.
Through thick and thin, she's always in my sight.
Darkness is cruel, but with her I see light.

This is a friendship that never goes in flames.
Our life is full of laughter, and games.
No matter what we're doing, no matter where we are,
Our friendship is forever, our friendship will go far.

I trust her with my secrets more than she can see,
I feel warm when she turns and says,
'Your secret's safe with me.'

She's never horrid nor bad, nor selfish nor mean.
She's the nicest friend there has ever been.
Once or twice with her I have wept
But as long as I know, my secrets are kept.

Sophie Marshall (12)
Port Glasgow High School, Port Glasgow

Irn-Bru Diamante

Irn-Bru
Great, tasty
Drink, pour, share
The best soft drink around
Play, laugh, create
Fun, pastime
Gaming.

Andrew Findlay McAllister (12)
Port Glasgow High School, Port Glasgow

Stolen

You took that
Something that I wanted to live myself
Something that makes me never want to forgive you
You stole my life
You stole my friends
You stole my job
You stole my style
You stole my life
I hope you know that you deserve your punishment
You deserve to feel the pain I felt
I went through torture
You crushed my soul
Why?
I've never done anything to you
So why did you do this to me?
My life was stolen by you.

Morgan Burns (12)
Port Glasgow High School, Port Glasgow

Dodgeball

Back and forth, back and forth, back and forth it goes.
Back and forth, back and forth, hitting someone on the nose.
Back and forth, back and forth, faster and faster it flies,
Back and forth, back and forth, glory is its prize.
Back and forth, back and forth, dodgeball is really fun,
Back and forth, back and forth, fun for everyone.

Scott David McAllister (12)
Port Glasgow High School, Port Glasgow

Football Skills

I kick the ball into the goal and the keeper falls, trying to reach for it.
Defenders try to tackle me,
I teach them how to be as good as me,
Midfielders trying to score, they just adore my tackles.
Strikers think they are good at skills,
Until they've seen my skills.

I score five goals and they start to dive,
Always onside, never offside.
All the managers want to sign me.
I make it look easy,
Are you dizzy yet, now excuse me,
I got more people to dominate,
'Cause this is my fate, to be the best,
I think you should have a rest now.

I'll put you to shame, make you stick to Xbox games.

Josh Harvey (12)
Port Glasgow High School, Port Glasgow

Autumn

A ll the leaves falling from the trees
U nder all the trees lies green glooming grass
T owers of trees covering the forest
U mbrellas catching leaves
M any colours and shapes
N ever a bit of green grass to see

S hades of orange, yellow and red
E verywhere you go
A nother leaf falls
S ome long, some short
O verlap as they fall
N ever forget the good times you had.

Rebecca Stevenson (12)
Port Glasgow High School, Port Glasgow

Winter Weather

W ater freezes to ice
I n the houses it's all warm and nice
N early everyone loves the snow
T he trees always glow
E very day fun
R ather the snow than sun

W inter is the best season
E xcited for a very good reason
A nother year of glistening snow
T omorrow it will be deeper I know
H urrying home to go out and play
E veryone knows more is coming our way
R eady for another day.

Abbie McKenzie (12)
Port Glasgow High School, Port Glasgow

The Old Firm Game

The old firm game
Rangers Vs Celtic
Green Vs Blue
All around the world
We've waited for this moment for years
And there sure will be tears
Explosions of green, storms of blue
Are all certainly due.
People chanting and ranting
Their songs of glory
At the home of one of the greatest games
To ever come to football
But it's not just a game
It's the battle of Glasgow.

Ross McVitie
Port Glasgow High School, Port Glasgow

Is This What Everybody Goes Through?

I do have a happy life,
I just don't feel it.
I know I don't have depression,
At home I'm fine.
I feel happier out of school,
Could it be school?

It gets you down when people are constantly finding problems,
Then nip away at you for.
Most of them are lies.
What's the point?

Constant arguing,
Rumours to riots,
Fibs for fights,
Forced friendships,
Is that what everyone goes through?

Even if it's not your problem,
It feels like it is,
You live through them all,
Stuck in a big group,
Should I speak up?

It piles up onto everything else,
You feel like you're going to break,
You learn to fight back the tears,
You let it out at home,
Where no one feels the need to judge you,
You feel like you can talk about it.
What about how Mum feels about it?

Mum wants to hear the highlights of the day,
But there are rarely any,
It's all nasty words,
Physical action,
Occasional threats,
Just negativity,
Should I stop talking about it?

Everyone assumes,

Never asks,
Risks the peace.
What about me?

People enjoy what others don't,
Wedge themselves into the cracks then slip out when they wish.
When things are picking up,
They drop back down,
What about the rest of the crowd?

Immaturity clashes with maturity,
Never slips past each other,
Some care,
Some don't.
Confidence clashes with shy.
Some don't speak up,
Some rise up too high.
What about both sides of the story?

They have popularity,
But they don't gain in the right way.
Maybe it's to do with their life at home.
Could it be bullying?

I don't know why some of it affects me,
Some people would find it silly,
Attention-seeking,
Could it be that you're guilty?

Poppy Waddington (13)
Rhosnesni High School, Wrexham

Nan

I love you Nan, you're the best,
That there could ever be,
I want to say, thank you Nan,
For all you do for me.

Thank you Nan, for all your love,
For having faith in me,
For taking the time to clear,
The things I didn't see.

Thank you for the good times,
The days you fill with pleasure,
Thank you for the memories,
And feelings that I treasure.

You're my up when I'm down,
The stars up in the sky,
You're the smile upon my face
And here's the reasons why . . .

You touch my life with kindness,
You know what I need,
Your caring nature shows so much
In every thought and deed.

Even through your tough times
And troubles that you've had,
You're still there for others
And to help you're always glad.

You've been through a lot in life,
I'm proud of who you are,
You're an inspiration,
You truly are a star.

You're our guardian angel,
To guide us through the years,
To give us your advice
And soothe away our tears.

You're our family guru,
You make our lives complete,
You're the centre of our world,
You keep us on our feet.

You're here for us when times are good
And when times are tough,
To say a great big thank you
Just doesn't mean enough.

To show you just how grateful
I really am to you,
I'm writing you this poem
And hoping it will do!

Chloe Griffiths (13)
Rhosnesni High School, Wrexham

Predators

Demons in human skin
Predators feeding on innocence
Tarmac hunting ground

They'll tear you up
Break you down
Spit you out

Break your mind
Break your soul
Break your bones

A gang of beasts
An easy prey
They make the kill

Teary face
Silver blade
Bleeding wrists

Their words
Are like knives
As they play with our lives

There's no point in talking
If no one hears the cry
Hurting, screaming, dying.

Jacob Burford (14)
Rhosnesni High School, Wrexham

It's All My Fault

It's my fault; it's always my fault,
Nothing was meant to happen,
You didn't have to retaliate,
You didn't have to fight,
You didn't have to haunt my dreams at night.

I couldn't stop my hands,
I couldn't stop my feelings,
I couldn't stop my heart from screaming,
But it didn't have to end like this,
We didn't have to meet each other's fists.

I couldn't stop the screaming,
I couldn't stop the shouting,
I couldn't stop the blaming,
But it didn't have to end like this,
We didn't have to meet each other's fists.

It's my fault; it's always my fault,
Nothing was meant to happen,
You didn't have to retaliate,
You didn't have to fight,
You didn't have to haunt my dreams at night.

I know I could've handled it better,
I know there were other ways,
Yet it felt so right at the time,
I could think of no other way to react,
I should have just left with my dignity intact.

We didn't need to get the cuts,
We didn't need the bruises,
We didn't need the wounds inside,
But I could think of no other way to react,
I couldn't have left with my dignity intact.

It's my fault; it's always my fault,
Nothing needed to happen,
I didn't need to start it,
I didn't have to fight,
And now it haunts my dreams at night.

Leah Edwards (14)
Rhosnesni High School, Wrexham

Potato Seed

Potato seed, potato seed,
Lovely, lovely potato seed,
Oh how I adore your magic,
Potato seed, potato seed,
With you in my life I am complete,
Potato seed, potato seed,
I watch your beauty grow day in day out,
Potato seed, potato seed,
Your plant growing so big,
Bringing beauty to my garden,
Potato seed, potato seed,
I watch over you like your family,
I protect you from all that wished you dead,
Potato seed, potato seed,
You're so big now,
You're starting to wither,
I don't think you will survive,
Until one day oh beautiful potato seed,
You grew into something extraordinary,
Something that will create my favourite snacks,
Potato seed, potato seed,
Crisps, chips, roast potatoes, so sweet to eat,
So I thank you,
Sweet potato seed,
Because without you,
My life would be incomplete.

Sophie Brightman (12)
Rhosnesni High School, Wrexham

Ghosts Of Memories

She walks with heavy steps,
As if tons of weights are on her shoulders,
Dragging her down.
The façade of a smile covering
The desperation, darkness, depression,
Of a trapped child in an unbreakable cage.
Cowering, cowering, locking herself away,
With a replica in her place.
Nobody can help her now.

She is known as the one whose smile doesn't reach her eyes,
The girl who skips to cover the drag.
The girl whose bright eyes started to fade,
Whose soft face turned sharp,
Whose smile turned into a grimace.

She used to be happy and loved,
But nobody saw behind the mask,
The pain, the torture,
The feeling of being alone in the world,
Nobody can help her now.

People say she ran off with a boy,
To make their own life but he devastatingly died.
People say she killed him in an act of bloodlust and desperation.
People say he used her.
People say she used him.
But they all know she loved him
And he broke her heart.

Everybody remembers that day,
The day the strong girl went weak.
They all blame it on the boy.
The boy who swaggered into her heart
And broke it from the inside.
She now builds her walls back up,
With stronger brick and stone than before.
Ghosts of memories pass through her face.
Nobody can help her now.

Bethan Ingman (12)
Rhosnesni High School, Wrexham

Life In A Book

Everyday life I read . . .
Day to day or year to year,
We can all give a cheer and read something.

Reading, reading, reading.

The words are like caterpillars, they turn into something beautiful.
Your eyes are wonderful things
Whether you need something to help you, you can still read.

Reading, reading, reading.

When I am in need of a helping hand
Or just something to pick me back up,
I can always rely on a character's help.
Even though they come from an author's head,
People always said you imagine.

Reading, reading, reading.

People can put you down but a book can turn your frown,
You imagine characters and are transformed
Into an imaginative world which is their home.
Paper is from trees and it turns into something on our knees.

Reading, reading, reading.

You can sit in silence, or in a loud area
But you can never be taken away
From that amazing world you are absorbed in.

Reading, reading, reading.

A story can be sad, happy or moving.
You will look into the depths of the author's thoughts,
Which will be your all-time favourite book.

Reading, reading, reading.

They start off as thoughts.
They look too big to read but are the best indeed.
It is a good thing to do and everyone knows it's true.

Reading, reading, reading.

Jessica Jones (13)
Rhosnesni High School, Wrexham

Crossy Road

Crossy Road,
Oh Crossy Road,
You're my favourite game.
I play you when I'm sad,
You're my escape from reality.
All the free gifts you give me,
Make me smile in delight,
Crossy Road, oh Crossy Road.

Crossy Road,
Oh Crossy Road,
I love you so.
Crossy Road, Crossy Road
I'm so glad I downloaded you.
That one day I was bored
So I looked on the app store
I then saw you.

Crossy Road,
Oh Crossy Road,
I read all your reviews,
All five stars so I downloaded you.
I've played you every day since.

Crossy Road,
Oh Crossy Road,
All the different characters you come with.
Poopy Pigeon, Disco Zoo,
Not forgetting the koala bear too.

Crossy Road,
Oh Crossy Road,
I love you so
Crossy Road, oh Crossy Road.

Rachel Hamlington (12)
Rhosnesni High School, Wrexham

Problems

Me, happy, joyful, full of hope,
Inside I'm crushed, almost broke.
Technology racing like a bullet,
Never keeping up.
New phone, not the best,
New clothes, worse than the rest.

Time racing, passing by,
School, exams, jobs.
Swimming through a sea of sorrow,
Carried by the tide.
Deadline days drawing nearer,
Never keeping up.

Family expect better,
Need to push for more.
Grades should be higher,
Achieve and soar.
All this pressure on me,
Never keeping up.

Questions scream, 'You know this!'
Yet answers stay dormant.
Brain slowly yielding,
To confusion and boredom.
Failure, not an option,
Never keeping up.

Appreciate achievement,
Celebrate success.
Hard work brings happiness,
Hope is helpless.
Excruciating effort,
You'll always keep up.

Benjamin Linney (13)
Rhosnesni High School, Wrexham

Temperantia Poem

How dare they do this,
He was innocent,
He didn't deserve it,
He was innocent,
They followed him,
And shouted things,
But still he was innocent.

He was walking home,
And they followed,
He was clueless,
But still they followed,
He looked back and then he knew,
But still, they followed.

'Where's Ethan?'
He ignored them,
'Aren't you mates?'
He ignored them,
'Where you going, off home?'
But still he ignored them.

He dropped to the floor,
They hit him,
He was in shock,
They hit him,
He refused to fight back, he was weak,
But still they continued to hit him.

He got up,
They left,
He watched him as they left,
Everyone was relieved that they left.

Lydia Wilding (12)
Rhosnesni High School, Wrexham

Fridge

I wander into the kitchen
And stop in front of the snowy white fridge
A smile slowly creeps across my face
Oh fridge!
Sweet precious fridge!
You keep things cool
But not too cold
You brighten up everyone's day
You are always there for me
Even on the harsh winter mornings
When I open the frosty white door
Your icy chill
Is always there to greet me
You look after our food and drinks
And ask for nothing in return
I slowly open the shiny white door
The light flickers
With a golden glow
Showing an amazing range of delights
Making the choice difficult
Which one of your gifts
Do I pick?
You're ever so important
Your job may seem simple
But no one else can do it
Oh fridge!
I don't know what I would do
Without you
Oh fridge!

Seren Prince (12)
Rhosnesni High School, Wrexham

Flour

Oh flour
How I adore you
You brought pizza into my life
You make my mealtimes happy
So I love you

Oh flour
I thank you for the pizza
It makes me have flavour explosions
With all your toppings that glisten like gems
Your stuffed crust like a river of gold
And your soft but crunchy base

Oh flour
To most people you are just crumbly white powder
But not to me, you have many different powers
You have brought light into my life
I can't imagine you not being here

Oh flour
You have also brought cakes into my life
I could not imagine my mealtimes
Without my cakes
The sweetness fulfils me
And the fairy cakes are like fairies granting me wishes
Your soft and spongy mixture is like a cloud of joy

Oh flour
You have brought happiness and power into my life
So I love you
Oh flour.

Megan Davies (13)
Rhosnesni High School, Wrexham

Cooking Chicken On The Hob

Oh chicken,
When I see you in the metal trolley,
I scream with delight
'It's chicken for tea!'
My eyes light up whenever I see you
And I beg Mum to cook you on the hob.
The sizzling noises you make,
Allow my tummy to rumble.
I think about how envious,
All the other children must be,
That I cook my chicken
On the hob!

When the flame ignites
I put the chicken on
And lick my lips,
Chicken is so delicious
I love how you taste,
Filling my mouth with such
A flavoursome sensation.
Some people think it is weird,
To cook chicken the way I do,
But I think that it is normal,
And the way you cook
Ever so slowly.

Isobel Teale Hayes (12)
Rhosnesni High School, Wrexham

Oh Chicken!

Oh chicken,
How I love to nibble on your bones,
Whilst taking selfies with you on my phone.
You have such a scented smell.
Oh chicken,
You're so fine,
Why make me wait in the long line?
Oh chicken,
Your friends are chips,
Tell them not to get salt on my lips.
Oh chicken,
I think I love you way too much,
I smile at the slightest touch.
I always visit your home in KFC
And take you home just for me.
Oh chicken,
Why have so many lush flavours,
Wing breast, fillet.
Oh chicken,
I despise sharing you with my friends,
Because they take you and the fun ends.
Oh chicken, juicy chicken,
I say goodbye until next time,
And you make me wait in the long line.

Morgan Rutter (13)
Rhosnesni High School, Wrexham

Bullying

The bullying online,
Happens all the time,
I stop and think,
Do I deserve it?

I pick up my phone
And see comments
With a horrible tone.
I throw it,
It crashes against the walls
And smashes as it falls.

I burst into tears,
Then fill with fears.
I think about what could come my way
And what they could say.

I come to school,
Not knowing what to do.
I act fine all the time
Even though I'm dying inside.

The bullying online
Happens all the time.
I stop and think,
Do I deserve it?

Holly Morris (13)
Rhosnesni High School, Wrexham

Ode To Unicorns

Oh unicorn,
Oh beautiful unicorn,
The layer of elegance that you wear
Is not at all rare,
It makes me want to stare all day,
If I don't I have to pay.
Oh unicorn,
Oh helpful unicorn,
Your heavenly eyes are enough to make the dead alive again,
Seeing you healing people gives me a 'nice' pain,
The fact you're attractive like any other is no lie,
It's something that makes me happy but cry.
Oh unicorn,
Oh wonderful unicorn,
The next prettiest thing about you is your magic,
That can kill any horrific tragic,
From your mane to your tail you are perfection,
But what really strikes me is your selfishness that has no rejection,
You are as precious to me as any valuable gem,
Not even the harsh thrones are going to break this rose stem,
Oh unicorn, I love you unicorn.

Arash Khangura (13)
Rhosnesni High School, Wrexham

Proud

This time I'll make you proud
To see me overcome all day life,
Proud of who you raised,
Your shelter, your peacefulness.

I'll make you proud,
Proud of who you raised up,
You know that I will always be
Here until the end.

Come back so I can say, thank you for this,
Home-cooked meals and a place to rest,
My troubled head when you're away,
I've passed the test, I've earned an A,
Not just in school but in life.

You'll always be right by my side,
To help me show, hope to all,
That are lost and sick in this dying world.

I'll use the love you left behind,
To change their minds,
I'll change their minds.

Rhys Evans (13)
Rhosnesni High School, Wrexham

If You Were Me

If you want to know
What it's like to be me
You have to deal with ADHD.

My name is Imogen
Sometimes I'm silly
But without my medication
I would be hyperactive.

ADHD is a disability
It's when you are hyper
I don't think that I'm different
I always think I have a super power.

When I was diagnosed with ADHD
I was only three
I started taking my medication
To help me calm down
Without that I would be bouncing off the ground.

This is me, a girl with ADHD
But I always thought that without it
I wouldn't be me.

Imogen Kavanagh (13)
Rhosnesni High School, Wrexham

An Ode To Music

Oh music, oh music
Without you not only my world is dull and boring
But the whole world.
You are poetry set to drums, guitar and a beat.
Oh music, oh music
If the world was an album
You're my favourite song.
I would listen to you all day long.

Catrin Francis (13)
Rhosnesni High School, Wrexham

An Ode To Roast Dinners

Oh roast dinners,
Without you Sundays would never be the same,
Your wonderful smells as you cook in the kitchen,
The steam that condenses my windows,
The strong smell of gravy,
The sound of vegetables boiling away,
Oh roast dinners,
The broccoli branches boiling in the saucepan,
The carrots that are like little pieces of sunshine,
The mashed potato like clouds covering my plate,
The rough and rocky roast potatoes like mini mountains,
Oh roast dinners,
The rich taste of gravy,
The variety of meat,
The broccoli branches like little trees,
Oh roast dinners,
Without your delicious taste,
My week is not complete.

Chloe Maddocks (13)
Rhosnesni High School, Wrexham

Pizza

Oh pizza, I love you.
You bring me so much joy and happiness in every piece.
Oh pizza, eating wouldn't be the same in my life without you.
You fill me with the nicest tastes like nothing else does.
You are the best food in the world.
Your taste is a cheese gold,
And your crust is the perfect addition.
If I didn't have you for my dinner sometimes
Everything would be so dull.
Thank you for being wonderful, oh pizza.

Ffion Roberts (13)
Rhosnesni High School, Wrexham

3DS

Oh 3DS,
You are as divine as the first sun of summer,
You are as fun as a night out on the town with Brian Blessed,
Yet you are as user-friendly as Darth Vader's voicemail message,
And you are way too expensive,
Seriously, why do you cost so much?

If I were without you 3DS,
My rainy weekend evenings would be mind-bogglingly dull,
My long plane/car trips would be unbearable,
My life would be without a Pokémon game with good graphics,
And I would not be able to see pictures I have taken in 3D!

My dear 3DS,
You are 'ice white' in your colour,
Yes you may look a bit flash,
But I wouldn't trade you for even a bundle of cash,
Well that's not true,
I would trade you for a big bundle of cash!

Leon Thomas (14)
Rhosnesni High School, Wrexham

Teenager

I feel confused, there's darkness all around
I don't know where to go
Should I run or face it?
I can't think straight
I don't know what's happening
Everything's changing so fast
I feel alone
Alone
A teenager.

Josh Duckett (12)
Rhosnesni High School, Wrexham

The Butterfly

Love is like a butterfly,
It goes where it pleases
And pleases where it goes.
It starts off as a caterpillar,
It turns so beautiful,
When it grows wings,
Happiness it brings.
See the colourful flowers,
It camouflages,
Flying around towers,
The colours are so bright,
Throughout day and night.
As it flies, through the city,
People stop and stare,
They say, 'Look at that
Beautiful butterfly over there.'

Rhiannon Major (12)
Rhosnesni High School, Wrexham

This Game Is Fantastic

Oh dear football
I love you
When your team finally wins
Inside you feel new
When you are in that stadium
Cheering on your team
Your stomach is buzzing
It feels like a dream
Whenever I play football
I'm always enthusiastic
This game brings out the best in me
I think it is fantastic.

Sam Ridgeway (14)
Rhosnesni High School, Wrexham

Humanchines

Their minds and bodies like bland machines,
In David Cameron's torn up kingdom
No emotion behind their eyes it seems,
When moving towards a greater freedom.

It's a terrible business politics.
Especially since you make enemies.
They use all of their conniving tactics,
And debate and argue, often with ease.

They don't answer questions with 'yes' or 'no'
So the public become disillusioned.
The fury of the public starts to grow,
When the politicians cause confusion.

Their promises to us are lacking pride.
So are they just taking us for a ride?

Daniel Gaughran (13)
Rhosnesni High School, Wrexham

Elephant

You are big
You are grey
You are what's known as a mammal.

You have big floppy ears
A long grey trunk
And four massive feet to be on your way.

All you eat are leaves and bushes
You can be found in a forest
A desert, maybe a savannah.

You are very intelligent
You can remember your way
Or so people say.

George Kavanagh (14)
Rhosnesni High School, Wrexham

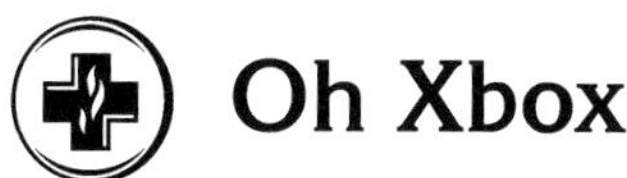

Oh Xbox

Oh Xbox
You're simply a god
The one and only
Xbox I love you
So great when giving me social connection with my mates
I wouldn't swap you for anything
Because of the huge mass of joy you bring
Oh Xbox you're a gaming sensation
Giving happiness to the nation
To me you're a king's crown jewel
And you're never mean or cruel
Xbox you're on my hall of fame
Without you I wouldn't be the same
Oh Xbox you're the best
You're as beautiful as birds hatching in a nest.

Luke Stamp (13)
Rhosnesni High School, Wrexham

Tomatoes For The Win

Oh tomato,
How I crave your taste,
How I'm constantly stuffing you in my face.
Without your amazing flavour,
I think I would change my behaviour.

When I eat you it's like a summer breeze,
It's almost like I'm up in the trees.
When I eat you I feel like a horse,
And without you we wouldn't have tomato sauce.

Without you I think that everyone would realise
That there is nothing about you they can despise.
Which brings me to the end of my letter,
That without you the world would certainly not be better.

William Taylor (13)
Rhosnesni High School, Wrexham

Nobody Knows

Nobody knows what it's like to be me,
Sometimes it's hard to be,
In my shoes and do what I do.

I have good times,
And bad times in my life,
Nobody knows what it's like to be me.

Questions run around my head,
Whilst I lay down in my bed,
Does anyone know what it's like to be me?

People don't always know what I'm thinking,
Am I happy?
Am I upset about something?

Nobody knows.

Joely Davies (13)
Rhosnesni High School, Wrexham

Life?

This is a life from its start till its nigh
His first breath that he shall not remember
The child's fun is full of parental lies
The fun in that best ever September
The sweet sixteen to the drunken eighteen
When him met her under the bright moonlight
She is his one and his only daydream
Nothing can break them, not even a fight
A man said to him life starts at forty
His childhood dream was lost in a past life
A long time ago he was quite naughty
What will wait for him in the afterlife?
Yet he didn't think his world was a lie
Unfortunately he has slowly died.

Jamie Jones (13)
Rhosnesni High School, Wrexham

Je Suis Charlie

On the 12th of January 2015
Paris experienced some terrible scenes.
Terrorists attacked all freedom of speech,
A worldwide security breach.
17 killed, that's many lives taken!
Europe is left disgusted and shaken.
Paris watches in shock and silence,
By cowards who only seek justice from violence.
Hostages are saved by unsung heroes,
They tried to keep the death toll at zero.
People attacked just as they shopped,
Racial attacks need to be stopped!
Cameron, Obama and the whole world unite,
We will give terrorism a fight!
We must be strong,
Terrorism is wrong.

Bethan Bloor (14)
Rhosnesni High School, Wrexham

Bullying

Watch them bully other people
Their stare, their look, their name-calling.
Feel the anger,
The shouting,
The fights.
The no money left,
The 'I got no stuff'.

Libby Hughes (12)
Rydal Penrhos School, Colwyn Bay

Death

I watered it with hope
Hid in its roots lies
Its leaves were my tears
Its branches my eyes

This tree grows old
And withers away
Yet you still water it
Every day

If this tree would die
Your woe would fade
Your life would be sunny
Out of the shade

Still you care for this tree
Use it as your shield
Hide under it
Your pain never yields

This tree locks you out
From all the world
Guards you tightly
And keeps you furled

And when you depart
From under that tree
Another takes your place
That person is me.

Millie Collins
Rydal Penrhos School, Colwyn Bay

Behind The Walls Of A Box

Behind the walls of a box,
I am safe and secure,
Behind that bright demeanour,
Grey side hides and follows . . .
The outer me is happy,
It is quite decisive,
It keeps inner me alone,
Inside darkness and warmth . . .
Inside the box here I lie,
Underneath doubtful fears,
But still here I am smiling,
Remembering back then . . .
Inside this ageing box here,
Contains wistful cards,
Images and photographs,
Here lays me in the past . . .
This box is still not full yet,
Although it has a lot,
I am still filling it up,
With logic and wisdom . . .
But when I do hide myself,
It's always with a smile,
I don't intend to trick you,
When I say it is real . . .

Kathleen Cheesley (13)
Rydal Penrhos School, Colwyn Bay

Every Time I See The Headlines

The world, full of kindness none of which gets seen.
Hate and cruelty are what we see and hear,
The news is all about the bad,
Why not talk about the good?
The frustration is added to,
Every time I see the headlines.
The venomous ivy of evil and hatred,
Is just being spread more and more.
We need positivity broadcast to us all.
Until then we have no hope.

Murder and death, who oh why?
The thought just makes me so angry.
Every time I see the headlines,
Something worse has happened.
The chance of seeing something good,
Isn't great at all
So I just get more frustrated.
Every time I see the headlines.

Eddie Farrell
Rydal Penrhos School, Colwyn Bay

Living In A Dream

I am in a dream and I hear a bang
I don't know what to do so I scream
The bang becomes louder and louder
I hide under my bed, scared and worried
I yell for my friend next to me, she doesn't answer
I turn her over and realise
She is dead!
The bang is so close to the door and I hide again
The bang stops
As I peer out I see a man with a big cane
He says, 'Run before they come'
'Who are they?' I ask who they are
He turns over with a horror face
I scream
I am wondering when this will ever end
Is it a dream?
Is it reality?
What's going on? Someone help me.

Amanda Sperring (11)
Rydal Penrhos School, Colwyn Bay

My Anger Fills Me

My anger fills me
It rages inside
The thought alone hurts
As though I'm about to die

My anger fuels me
For everything day in, day out
But I do know
It's nasty throughout

My anger comes randomly
It almost confuses me
It's just a bad mood
My anger has no end

I can't control it
It made me sad
Anger pushes me
Is anger so bad?

Abhishek Bathula
Rydal Penrhos School, Colwyn Bay

The Hypocrite

The politicians, sitting in their fancy cars and talking about helping the poor.
The politicians, who spend their day arguing about why they are the best,
While the heroes of the country die on the streets.
The politicians, who waste thousands of pounds on their grabs for power,
While people die of a disease that just a few pennies could help stop.

The royals, lazing around in their undeserved palace of gold.
The royals, taking money from those who they do nothing for,
While minorities are slaughtered across the world.
The royals, who pretend to fight while protected by a hundred men,
While civilians die thanks to a lack of troops.

The ordinary people, who sit and write about how the rich do nothing.
The ordinary people, who have fallen to a schedule of work, eat and sleep,
While millions pray for a scrap of food every day.
The people like me, who talk about how bad the world is and do nothing about it,
While our world slowly falls to a dark, dark place.

Edward Patrick (13)
Rydal Penrhos School, Colwyn Bay

Ditched

Where do I go?
Me and you is a lifetime ago,
Time is slow,
I am having permanent vertigo,
In school I'm sitting alone,
Just texting my bro,
Living life solo,
Can't wait till I get home,
Just spend my life on my phone,
You threw me so low,
Watched you at the top while I was below,
But it's too hard to let go,
I was falling but I didn't realise,
It was you who had grown,
And the worst thing is -
This is not my fault!

Saskia Schmidt (12)
Rydal Penrhos School, Colwyn Bay

Encompassing Love

Why is love confined
To a man and woman thing?
Why are you against the mix
That human life can bring?

Why do you hate those who don't
Just swing your way?
All have the right to happiness
Don't take their right away.

Being homophobic
Is now a social taboo
If you choose to come out
How would they treat you?

Tallulah Batley (13)
Rydal Penrhos School, Colwyn Bay

Cancer

As I stare out the world becomes a blur,
I wait and hope that I am in a nightmare,
But I am not,
I can hear the clock ticking as I sit and wait,
Wait for something good to happen in my life,
But nothing happens,
Suddenly there is a knock at the door,
'I am safe,' she says, 'it has gone,
The cancer has gone!'
I feel like a wave has just washed away all of my fears and worries,
I cry tears of happiness and give her a hug,
These past few months have been so grey,
But finally I can say hooray,
So even though she nearly lost her life,
It has taught me a valuable lesson,
You only live once so make he most out of it!

Natalie Lever
Rydal Penrhos School, Colwyn Bay

Travel

To travel is to fly,
An endless journey,
An endless flight,
To soar over the land.

To travel is to sail,
A journey of ups and downs,
A journey of water,
To sail through the sea.

To travel is to walk,
A path with different terrains,
A path of hard work,
To stroll through this world.

Adrian Lewis (12)
Rydal Penrhos School, Colwyn Bay

Suffragettes

'Suffragettes, Suffragettes' in the air,
'Suffragettes, Suffragettes' watch and stare,
We watched them walk down the street,
Shouting about women's rights to everyone they meet,
Banners flying everywhere,
And sirens sounding in the air,
Then the police came in a flash,
Then there was a massive crash,
The police pulled some away,
As they shouted, 'This is downplay,'
Some were taken to prison,
But it still didn't change their decision,
I looked, they made no struggle,
They looked as if they were in trouble.

Luiza Gratton (11)
Rydal Penrhos School, Colwyn Bay

What It Is Like – Haiku

My heart's beating fast,
Excitement rushes through me,
What will happen next?

Raha Aminnejad
Rydal Penrhos School, Colwyn Bay

Mirror

I watch the wall,
Staring at me,
Glaring in my direction,
Straight at my face.

I've fallen to pieces,
Finding myself,
Amongst the surface,
Glimmering in sadness.

I reclaim my feet,
Take one more glimpse,
Before turning and running,
Back to Mother and Father,
Away from that mirror . . .

Samuel Jones (13)
Rydal Penrhos School, Colwyn Bay

Till The End

My emotions are the oceans
Crashing wave upon wave
The wind are my feelings
Lingering in the air
The Earth understands me
The one who cares
The fire is my soul
The one in pain
And then there's you
My loving friend
The one who's there
With me
Till the end.

Bijou Rajagopal
Rydal Penrhos School, Colwyn Bay

Triumph

We won of course
This time the referee wasn't yours
Speed, skill aggression
The Ruthin parents felt depression

Mold led from the start
Every player playing their part
They said it was unfair
But with an independent ref, we didn't care

Power and bulk never beat skill and pace
So we restored our pride
At Mold Rugby Club, our base

But there's no bad karma
Because as RGC East
We'll be the best
When at Under 15s together we play RGC West.

William Roberts (13)
Rydal Penrhos School, Colwyn Bay

Festive Times

In the house. Cosy and warm
Me, Mum, Dad and Paula
Christmas tree, bright and magical
Rustling, cheerful chatting, pots bubbling
Soup, cinnamon and spice and everything nice
Delighted, loved, treasured.

Denise Reid
South Lanarkshire College, East Kilbride

Dissimilis

I'm a mistake?
I can't do that?
You think you know me?
I think you're mistaken
How do you know I can't do that?
You don't know me
Because I'm not you
I can do things you can only dream of.
I change like the wind, first going this way then going that way
I rise like an eagle rocketing toward the sky
And I dive back down to the Earth
As everyone else stares at me
I am free
Free to be whatever I want to be while you are stuck
Stuck to be just one thing
Stuck to be just brave and never have fear
Stuck to be a genius and never be wrong
But me
I am free
Free to be brave
Free to be scared
Free to be a genius
Free to be wrong
I am free
You are trapped
I am Dissimilis.

Christopher Howie
South Lanarkshire College, East Kilbride

The Prosecution

Life is a court room
I am the prosecutor
And the world is the judge
I must point out the lies to show the truth
In a world where lies are seen as the truth
Others try to deceive me and take me away from the truth
But I must stay focused for myself
To truly see the lies in front of me
For the world is truly beautiful
For when all lies are gone
The beautiful truth is seen through
For this is my dream
An honest dream
For a world covered in lies
Can be beaten by the hopeful truth of an honest person
Now the prosecution is ready your honour.

Connor Larkin
South Lanarkshire College, East Kilbride

Carpe Diem

No lifetime is long. It is way too short.
Every day your life gets shorter.
So live it to the full.
Seize the day.
Carpe Diem.

Zak McKenna (12)
Stirling High School, Stirling

Love

L ove is an amazing thing
O pen your mind to it
V oyage its seas
E nter its world of dreams.

Christopher Allan O'May (12)
Stirling High School, Stirling

I Can't Think

At this blank page I stare
With nothing to write.
As I look at clear air
No thought is in sight.

I've tried and I've tried
But to my mind nothing has come.
I must hurry there's a deadline
But ideas, I have none.

My head full of nothing.
My pencil just moves.
Think, I must write something
But my brain will refuse.

As the clock ticks by
There are some words on my page
Come on, I must try
To get over this phase.

There's a blank page no more
But a poem of mine.
No more stress, just relief for
I have completed it on time.

Holly Davis (13)
The Royal High School, Edinburgh

The Seasons

I sit on the wall
And watch the autumn leaves fall
Autumn is in full swing
I hear the birds sing

Frost covers the ground
Christmas is coming around
The cold winter chill
Brings a thrill

Flowers are blooming
Hay fever sufferers are fuming
Baby animals are being born
Farmers are harvesting their corn

The hot sun is beaming down
The blazing heat hits the town
The water is sparkling
The nights are shortening

These are the seasons.

Lauren Pollock (13)
The Royal High School, Edinburgh

Dreaded Dreams

Dark thoughts and dark dreams,
The night is now darker than it seems.
They chase you, you shout, you sweat, you run;
You're trapped . . . no one can hear you, no one.
You wish there was a way they could leave your mind; disappear,
You can't face the days without some hint of fear.
They won't let you wake up, 'Stay asleep, stay asleep!'
Your bed is the ocean, filled with the tears you weep.
No matter how long you try and stay awake,
They will always be there, they will always wait.

Katie McKenzie (13)
The Royal High School, Edinburgh

The Seasons' Bells

The ever-changing seasons bring their wrath,
When winter comes around and brings its chill,
We see in the air our lingering breath,
Our spirits winter's monster will not kill.

Then, somehow the icy blanket will lift,
Bringing freshly grown flowers and new life,
Spring is now calling, the seasons now shift,
Clashing of weather, that's helping life thrive.

Earth's beauty shines through, bringing new creatures,
The sun gaining powers, light shining through,
Earth now bringing all of summer's features.

The last transaction, bringing something new,
Red, orange, yellow, drowning Earth's soil,
Trees are now empty; Earth's beauty is spoilt.

Lara Teden (13)
The Royal High School, Edinburgh

The Hatred

Secrets and lies create upmost despise,
I see no kindness, looking into your eyes.
Hatred so strong, I feel something's wrong,
Not all can be fixed with a sad love song.

Secrets and lies, the cause of goodbyes,
Your anger like thunder, reflecting the sky.
Heart as cold as stone, chills me to the bone,
How do I trust you when picking up the phone?

Secrets and lies, oh how time does fly,
Not long ago, my life was on a high -
Your face alone, a great work of art,
The beauty of hatred will break your heart.

Maisie Evans (13)
The Royal High School, Edinburgh

Lies

Oh, you'll regret those words!
Give back my heart and take my hate instead,
Was it my enemy or my friend I hurt?
What a brave heart for such a little head.

Come and I will show you my newest flat,
And you may watch me purse my mouth and blink,
Oh, I shall love you still and all of that,
I never now will tell you what I think.

I shall be crafty and sly, soft and sweet,
You will not catch me speaking anymore,
You shall never hear a single peep
And some day when you push the door.

A sane day, not too calm and not too stormy,
I may be gone and you can whistle for me.

Laura Morris (14)
The Royal High School, Edinburgh

A Deadly Choice

One cigarette, that was all,
That was all it took as I recall,
I still see those flames even to this day,
When I close my eyes they will not go away.

So fearless they were, growing higher and higher,
It did not stall, this raging fire,
The screams of women could be heard for miles,
When the building burnt down, tile by tile.

The tears of loved ones could fill a lake,
Because of the risk I choose to take,
For the rest of my life I will regret,
Lighting that deadly cigarette.

Charlie Ashcroft (13)
The Royal High School, Edinburgh

Winter Calls

The seasons are changing ever so fast,
Orange and reds quickly fading away,
The changing of seasons seems ever so vast,
Nature evolves by seasons every day.

Winter calls as the days are shortening,
The crisp cold air nipping at my toes,
Glittering grass fresh in the morning,
Sun beams melting thick layerings of snow,
Winter's night lays down a blanket of
Freezing fresh snow at the crack of dawn.

Winter fades as spring brings its creatures,
Vibrant and bursting with new colours ablaze,
Showing off its beautiful features,
Brighter and brighter with the coming of days.

Erin Brown (13)
The Royal High School, Edinburgh

Cabbage And Ribs

It's match day and Easter Road is bouncing.
The two teams begin to leave the tunnel.
And the Hibs fans were about to sing,
'We are the Hibees and we're from Easter Road'.
The game is about to get underway,
A cheeky little touch from Malonga,
They lose the ball but Hearts don't want to play.
Hibs' fans start to do the conga,
For Dominique Malonga,
Who plays a pass to Paul Hanlon,
He takes a touch and finds Scott Allan's feet,
An early cross from Cummings was neat.
The timid Hearts' defence were hiding,
Do Doo Doo Dominque Malonga.

Rory Campbell (13)
The Royal High School, Edinburgh

The Rugby Pitch

The ball is thrown, across the rugby pitch
The players are in anticipation.
Flashbacks to training, running through a ditch
Within the players; communication.
All of the player's minds are connected
The number 10 catches the ball, and runs
He's the captain, whom teammates elected
You can tell they are all having great fun.

The long 80 minutes, are almost done
The ref begins, to pull out his whistle
He blows it, and the sound is like a gun
The sound pierces ears as clear as crystals.
The players line up, and start to shake hands
The scoreboard is shown, across the whole land.

Lewis Trundle (13)
The Royal High School, Edinburgh

Cleaning

After the biggest dinner of my life,
Now begins the cleaning and the strife.
Walking around this house trying to clean,
But after this clean is only a dream.
Getting out the Hoover and hoovering,
Getting the brush and broom and sweeping.
Trying and trying to clean up the sick,
Sawdust and cinnamon sure does the trick.

Finally when the cleaning is over,
I lay down to rest and try to sleep.
I dream of picking a four-leaf clover,
And cleaning up this mess and . . . *Beep! Beep!*
I wake up and think, *thank god it's done,*
To clean up after Thanksgiving is really no fun.

Julian Moller (14)
The Royal High School, Edinburgh

Joy

Golden face waking to a day of new.
Her shining beams that give the world its light
Revealing a glistening blanket of blue.
A natural alarm clock that wakes us from night.
The day brings trouble that can be overcome.
Listen to people who say, 'Don't lose hope'
There's always someone there when you're all done.
Or perhaps someone throwing you the rope.

If you love someone then they are a part
Of your life that you will never forget.
Everyone has someone that's in their heart
Life with love is a life without regret
Like a child receiving the gift of a toy,
Our world has an abundance of joy.

Rachel Sunter (13)
The Royal High School, Edinburgh

Ongoing War

Where is dignity when death relieves the pain?
No memory of those who live terminal,
Nor candles lit for those who die in vain,
Victims who suffer and are no colonel,
Yet they have the fight of Roman legends,
On an edge yet they're only edging,
Life is one struggle after another,
There is no time for desperate cover.

But sympathy will not heal the sickened,
Only drive the sick to their patient foe,
Their resounding innocence takes the blame,
For there is no fairness with all the death,
Yet there is never sanity through the
Inevitable bringing the silence.

Daniel Harrison (13)
The Royal High School, Edinburgh

Losing The Unknown

A bullet whizzes past, a train above my head,
As I stand in a field covered in blood.
My friend lies on the ground, sporting a hole filled with lead.
As I wash my shoes, brown with mud.
The image stays in my head, making me scream.
The wail of pain and a bang is all I hear.
My sanity is tearing at the seams,
My mind is jumbled, nothing is clear.

The sun sets, leaving me in the dark.
Shutting the curtains in my mind.
These days will surely leave a mark and
I hope to one day put this all behind.
One day this war will surely be won,
But I will remain in the dark, never seeing the sun.

Megan Ramage (13)
The Royal High School, Edinburgh

The Ocean

Calm and gentle, the ocean can be,
Water flowing softly, with subtle grace.
Perhaps raging and fierce? A sight to see.
Rushing so fast, impossible to chase.
Boats swaying in the distance, to and fro
As the waves jump and rush fast toward the shore.
What lies beneath it, I will never know,
The deep blue ocean hides secrets and more.

Waves jumping and crashing, rushing so fast,
Racing over the sea like white horses.
The ocean is large and ever so vast,
With the entirety nature's forces.
Colours and patterns of beauty so great,
What magical things the ocean creates.

Laura Harris (13)
The Royal High School, Edinburgh

Metamorphosis

In summer – white chocolate, sweet and pure.
Slipping through the fingers, melting away.
For some the illness, for other's the cure.
In autumn – a sunset, closing the day.
My final moments burning away but
Beauty is found as I fade into night.
In winter – closed doors and curtains drawn shut.
Alone and getting weaker as I fight
A life or death battle I keep losing.
In spring – a phoenix, I rise from the earth.
Out of the dirt, like the new sun pushing
Though the clouds. My miracle, my rebirth.

Seasons keep changing, my current shape shifts,
From sweet to bitter or from drops to lifts.

Emma Walker (13)
The Royal High School, Edinburgh

Arsenal

There is a famous club from Emirates,
They had not won a cup in eight long years;
Arsene Wenger was keeping the team fit,
They thought it was going to end in tears,
The match was underway, the teams start to play.
Olivier Giroud started with the ball,
Arsene Wenger was about to say,
Stay on your feet and don't fall.
In ten minutes Arsenal go two-nil down,
Aaron Ramsey sends the ball wide.
Arsene Wenger begins to frown,
Per gets the ball the defender doesn't hide.
Free kick, Santi Cazorla shoots the ball,
'Doo, Doo, Doo, Santi Cazorla' they call!

Jamie Cunningham (14)
The Royal High School, Edinburgh

Nazi Deserter

My heart is a drum beating in the heat
My head is a target frozen in time
My hands hold a metal killer hiding in the wheat
My body shouldn't be here I feel like a crime
My legs are quivering I slowly step onward
My eyes like telescopes searching the forest
My gun is ready barrel aimed forward
A sudden bang sends a chill from the forest
A tiny iron fist pushing through my chest
A desperate cry for help yet none will arrive
My lungs bowing down, knowing who's best
My heart slowing down, this song's almost over
My body keeling over coming to a rest
My ears hear torture, the laughing over and over.

Connor Coull (13)
The Royal High School, Edinburgh

The Guilty

Drip, drip, drip, drip,
No one can ever know,
Drip, drip, drip, drip,
He was neither friend nor foe.

The blood that's dripping off my hands,
Will never wash away,
Drip, drip, drip, drip,
The stains are here to stay.

The guilty voices in my head,
Get louder every day,
Saying I killed an innocent man,
And I will have to pay.

Katie Hepburn (13)
The Royal High School, Edinburgh

Dulce Et Decorum Est

(Inspired by 'Dulce Et Decorum Est' by Wilfred Owen)

Lines in double, slept as beggars inside sacks
Knocking knees, we go through the sludge.
Lines in forward, polished shoes and pressed backs
Gallop forward, the canon's trudge.
Through the smoke, waves the flags
Horses charge, squares are formed.
Enemy flees as beaten stags
Those who fall shall be mourned.

Collapsing into the sea of green
Reloading upon order, in bags we are fumbling.
Gracious lines, neatest uniforms you've ever seen
Backward, the wounded are stumbling.
Those unready are shot in the chest
Ah the sweet cries of Dulce Et Decorum Est
Pro Patria Mori.

Angus Walker Stewart (13)
The Royal High School, Edinburgh

Wolfie

It takes one to see the full moon,
One to see the fire,
One to hear the howls,
But takes many to see the reality,
Fatality,
And formality of this world,
But if one can take down the world,
Then many shall make it rise,
We see the moon and think,
See the fire and fear,
Hear the howls and see the wolf,
But nobody sees the wolf in me,
Feels the fire seep through me
And hears the howls pierce the night that is nigh.

Freya Marshall (12)
Westmuir High School, Glasgow

Kaayaan

Coming to Britain because of battle
Home was invaded by evil tyrants
The soldiers that fought, their weapons did rattle
So he got up and left

Became a victim of racial abuse
Small-minded thug that did not know the facts
Upon him a weapon this racist did use
On the stairs to his home

He could not believe this happened to him
So angry he wanted to murder this thug
His thoughts had begun to become rather grim
Then the letter arrived

Suit had been purchased
Lawyer has been hired
Face has been shorn
Has driven to court

Standing in the witness box feeling down
He sees the jury whispering so soft
That many emotions he thinks he'll drown
Then forgiveness hit him.

Regan McIlmoyle (14)
Westmuir High School, Glasgow

Things We Call Ourselves

I wish I was an honest man to do the best I can
I wish I was an angel trustworthy as can be
I wish I was harmonious to prevent the wars
Peace is all the world wants and needs
Let no man bleed for humour or culture.

I wish I was a turtle, thick-skinned and wise
Smaller and stronger than everybody else
Outcast because of his height
Thick skin doesn't take in the laughter, it blocks it out
Hardest of us all the mighty turtle.

I wish I was a boxer, agile as can be
Dodging all the abuse and putting these words to good use
I wish I was dedicated or just better educated
Confident in what I'm doing, work or pleasure there's no pressure.

I wish I was a traveller seeing all four corners of the globe
Information gathering, couldn't do it quick enough
I wish I was full of adventure then maybe I wouldn't be an outsider
I wish, I wish, I wish I was still in my bed.

Bradley Seager (14)
Westmuir High School, Glasgow

We Scots

David Cameron ya think yir very wide
Am gonnaae tell ya no so ya better back off
Wae yir daft Tory party so go away
Or ah'm gonna dae something about it
Cause ah'm no gonnae greet like a wee wean
Wae nae teddy so you better let become independent
Cause I don't want to be stuck wae red, white, blue
For the rest of our life
We Scots want blue and white
But unfortunately ya said naw so ah'm no happy
Other people ir no happy an aw
We Scots fight for our freedom and die for our country
But David Cameron you and yir daft wee speeches
We Scots are no liking yir patter
We Scots aren't gonnae gie up we are gonnea come back and boot you in the bahookie
So you better watch yir back cos we Scots are wee sneakies
We are gonna become independent one day and yir no gonna stop us Scots
So ya better run.

Liam McLachlan (15)
Westmuir High School, Glasgow

The Shock!

I walked over to Anya
She was in bed
There she lay
Still and dead!

I shouted for help
I didn't know what to do
I picked up the phone
And called my best friend Sue.

I told her what happened
That Anya was dead
She said, 'Wait, I'll be there,
Just stand by her bed.'

Finally, yes Sue is here
She said, 'Call Anya's mum
She should be near.'

I called Anya's mum
She said there is nothing we can do
She asked who I was with
I replied, 'My best friend Sue.'

Anya's mum is here
Anya was in bed
Then Anya moved
Anya was not dead!

Llinos Hill (12)
Ysgol Eirias, Colwyn Bay

Our World

There is a light outside every window
And every moment someone puts up a fight,
Another bird of opportunity takes flight,
Cries of, 'Je suis Charlie,' fill the street,
It makes someone's day if you are sweet,
For any moment your world could shatter,
Into millions of pieces everywhere
And when you get them back
You discover some aren't even there,
We all need someone to be sweet,
When our world is not so sweet,
As guns fire in cities
There are so many who pity,
But look as if they do not care,
There are tears of sadness everywhere,
As the whole world descends into madness,
Although some don't think it's their fight,
Everybody should have their rights,
The pen is mightier than the sword,
Just make sure you use it the right way,
You may not receive a punishment today,
But there will certainly be something
Waiting for you the next day,
It could only be 24 hours away
And it can all happen in a blink of an eye.

Grace Wilkinson
Ysgol Eirias, Colwyn Bay

Mazes

I've spent most of my days drifting, searching
My mind in a blank trance,
Searching for who I could be,
But no one knows.

If I carry on walking
I might find a light,
I'll follow it until it stops
But then what?

Don't pretend to be her, or her,
Just be you and only you
And you will emerge from darkness
And find yourself smiling.

Don't search for someone who you
Feel like you have to pretend.
Search for that one who
Loves you for you.

I know it's boring, tiring,
But when it all stops,
When you find you,
There will be another maze ahead.

Ellie Grace Willet (12)
Ysgol Eirias, Colwyn Bay

The Rough Society We Live In

Why are children treated like they're unwanted and small?
Why are adults treated like they're wise and tall?
Why can't people see how good children can be?
Why do adults take drugs and think it's good for thee?
Why do adults smoke and think it's OK?
Do they ever think it will give them cancer one day?
Why are the places children grow up really rough?
It makes growing up for them really tough.

No one knows the anger and loneliness that they go through.
No one knows they get laughed at because their things are old not new.
It makes me so angry that children always show a tear
Because they get laughed at as they live in a place full of nasty people to fear.

Why don't we help the lonely child
And not keep our distance as if they're an animal from the wild.
You know exactly who I mean.
The one who is always at the back trying not to be seen.

So why don't you help them there and then
And do a simple thing like giving them a pen?
Why don't you do as I say?
Why don't you want to give a child a brighter day?

Rosie Fox (12)
Ysgol Eirias, Colwyn Bay

The Zoo

We look at them through the bars.
The bars that contain them.
We stop and stare
But not aware
What anger lies within them.
It must be sadness and rage
At a young age.
But deep down there is a spark
That shimmers and glimmers in the night,
Which lifts them up with light.
With so much joy,
Like a 15-year-old boy
Who found the love,
The love of his life.
His love is limited
But not for much longer.
There are some
Who want things to be done
About this sadness,
This rage and madness.

Iwan Edward John Jones (12)
Ysgol Eirias, Colwyn Bay

Joy

J oy, nothing can annoy when you feel joy
O thers can't enjoy the simple things like playing with a toy
Y ears go by like tears fading away, lying back in the hay

E very day I just like to play
N othing can stop me I am so happy
J ust the thought of ice cream and pancakes
O nly makes me more excited
Y esterday on the 3rd of May my birthday.

Christian D'Angelo (11)
Ysgol Eirias, Colwyn Bay

The Devil In Me

As my face becomes red,
An agony throbbing through my head,
Creating a whirlwind inside of me,
Letting all the anger be free,
Dragging darkness and shadows into my soul,
Turning me to be sharp and cruel.

Flooding into me is all the hate,
Making me want to burst into flames,
A large pointed red tail starts to form,
Giving me two wings and two horns,
The Devil in me is coming out,
Ready to flare all about.

I begin to spread my gloom and sadness,
While the town is full of madness.
A whirlwind I create full of tears,
While everyone gasps with fear.
I am the Devil!
I am here!

Teigan Elspeth Crees-Jones (12)
Ysgol Eirias, Colwyn Bay

Starlight Beauty

Flowing mane, silky tail,
Galloping through the night,
Silhouetted against the sky so pale,
Following the path of light.
You are a beauty, my only dream,
My lovely horse, my wonderful girl.
Neighing like a nightingale.
You are a horse, I am a teen.
Your eyes are like two shining pearls
And I will now pass on your tale.

Beth O'Rourke (12)
Ysgol Eirias, Colwyn Bay

Dance Is Love, Dance Is Life

Dance means a lot to me,
I do it three times a week.
I have contemporary on Tuesday,
Hip hop on Wednesday
And modern/tap on Thursday.

Leotard and leggings are what we wear,
They're alright to wear I guess that's fair.
We do a show every other year
With exams in-between.

Dance means a lot to me
I do it three times a week.
My dance squad are always up for a laugh
And are there for me when I'm sad.

Dance means a lot to me
I do it three times a week.
No one can take it away
Because it is in my heart to stay.

Sioned Caddick (12)
Ysgol Eirias, Colwyn Bay

The Shoes

They lay there, on the
Road.
Casting crimson shadows larger than their
Bodies.
Friendly faces fixate upon a
Tragic tableau.
Their heels away from traffic, their owner
Away.

What is 40 to 30?
A life's difference.

Jordan Harding (16)
Ysgol Eirias, Colwyn Bay

Raging Fire

The raging fire in my soul
Is burning all night,
The death, the destruction, the horribleness
It makes me want to fight.

I shout, I scream, I hope,
I hope that it would all end.
But what I do not realise
Is what's around the bend.

Suddenly, out of nowhere
A bomb drops out of the sky,
I now know it's time
To make my last goodbye.

The raging fire in my soul
Is burning all night,
The death, the destruction, the horribleness
It makes me want to fight.

Iwan Woodhead (11)
Ysgol Eirias, Colwyn Bay

War

Life or death in a blink of an eye,
Will you survive or will you die?
Gun shells and explosions going off everywhere.
All full of fear
Are those who fight or go in flight.
Most people will die on that fatal night.
You can't deny, you are scared,
Are you ready or are you unprepared?
You all should be scared!

Joe Smith (11)
Ysgol Eirias, Colwyn Bay

Second Chances

I'm water that flows softly,
But not all the time,
Sometimes I rage roughly,
Sometimes I let out a whine.

Similar to people I suppose,
Some people are gentle,
Some people like to doze,
And even people go mental.

A river flows through stops and starts
Like people with their shopping carts,
A river has its ups and downs,
Like people who make everybody frown.

All I can say
Is that people should pay
For all the wrong they have done in their life
Like murdering someone or divorcing your wife.

Luke Benn (13)
Ysgol Eirias, Colwyn Bay

Jokes

There are different types of jokes
For different types of people.

And there are different kinds of laughs
For different kinds of people.

Some may smile
Every once in a while.

A baby may smile
After crying for a while.

But a joke about someone is different
From their point of view.

And when the boot is on the other foot . . .
You will see it too!

Brooke Japheth (13)
Ysgol Eirias, Colwyn Bay

Monsters

Small and irritating,
They really put you in a mood.
They will find a way
To get under your skin.
You can run
But you can't hide.
They're always there,
They're always here.
They will drive you round the bend,
It will never end.

They lurk under your bed,
Maybe in the wardrobe.
It gives you nightmares
And sometimes daymares.
It will make you cry and scream,
You could rip your hair out, it's so mean . . .

Cameron McQueen (12)
Ysgol Eirias, Colwyn Bay

Modern Life

This life is filled with death and destruction,
This started with the Earth's construction,
When supplies were scarce,
But rich people thrived,
This is when rebels began to arrive.

They would fight for money and appreciation,
The rich would fight back to defend their nation,
But the rebels would attack constituencies,
Making the rich fall down to their knees,
This is why armies are needed
To do what is pleaded,
Bringing death and war!

Morgan Simmonds (12)
Ysgol Eirias, Colwyn Bay

Just Love

OK . . . so here goes,
I don't know how to say this but . . .
You are the apple of my eye,
The Peter to my Pan,
The Never to my Land,
The Captain to my Hook,
The lily to my pad,
The beat to my heart,
The blue to my sky,
The words to my book,
The Mamma to my Mia,
The lyrics to my song,
The line to my paper
And the ink to my pen.
Just one simple question,
Will you go out with me?

Elin Haf Jones (12)
Ysgol Eirias, Colwyn Bay

Friendship

Me and my friend
Are so much alike.
Me and my friend
Will never fight.

Sometimes I wonder
If my friend is real.
In a dream she was
My mirror.

I am sure she can grant wishes,
For she has granted one of mine,
To be the best of all friends,
My guardian angel.

Sophie Brown (12)
Ysgol Eirias, Colwyn Bay

Love

Love is all around you,
Even in the air,
You see it right beside you,
As you do your hair.

You look at their picture every day,
You talk to them online.
You walk up to them to talk to them
But then you turn away.

You finally have the guts
But then he doesn't turn up.
Try tomorrow,
Another day,
Will you ever give up?

Verity Stenson
Ysgol Eirias, Colwyn Bay

It's A Hard Life!

It's pretty hard to be me,
If only you could see,
You think it's all fun and games,
But you're wrong, actually!
My parents split up,
I left my friends,
My sisters drive me round the bend!
Life is hard, I have to admit,
But I grit my teeth and get on with it.
If I were you and you were me, only for a day,
Well then you would see,
What it's like to be me,
Not easy is it, eh!

Claire Dennison (12)
Ysgol Eirias, Colwyn Bay

The Battle Began

In 1066 the battle began
William was a well-organised man
To get back his crown was his plan
He arrived with his army well equipped and strong
Harold thought his army was better but he was wrong
The bloodshed was about to start
William's men look like they were about to depart
William's men shot an arrow up from up high
Harold got shot in the eye
What a horrible way to die
William's men began to sing
For their leader was going to be king.

Connor Workman (13)
Ysgol Eirias, Colwyn Bay

Feelings

My life at home is tough,
Sometimes it gets rough.
It was extra hard when my mum broke her leg,
Then I had to care for my sister instead.
My dad leaves for work at half seven,
He has to be there for eight,
He spends ten hours working,
Then he goes out for a drink.
I have three pets at home,
Their names are Trixie, Oscar and Ghost,
I have to take Trixie for a walk
And then feed all three when I get home.

Megan Jones (12)
Ysgol Eirias, Colwyn Bay

Memories

As I walk through the darkness of my past
A bomb of memories burst.

From the good to the bad,
They all make me sad.

From the old to the new
It will always be about me and you!

A pool of light started to appear,
Then I thought you were actually here.

I never knew you could be this far,
Because our friendship is the best and strongest I know.

Paigelouise Fitzgerald (12)
Ysgol Eirias, Colwyn Bay

YOUNG WRITERS INFORMATION

We hope you have enjoyed reading this book – and that you will continue to in the coming years.

If you're a young writer who enjoys reading and creative writing, or the parent of an enthusiastic poet or story writer, do visit our website **www.youngwriters.co.uk**. Here you will find free competitions, workshops and games, as well as recommended reads, a poetry glossary and our blog.

If you would like to order further copies of this book, or any of our other titles, give us a call or visit **www.youngwriters.co.uk.**

Young Writers,
Remus House
Coltsfoot Drive,
Peterborough,
PE2 9BF

(01733) 890066 / 898110
info@youngwriters.co.uk